VALLEY
OF
SORROW

VALLEY OF SORROW

A LAYMAN'S GUIDE
TO UNDERSTANDING
MENTAL ILLNESS

ALEXANDER B. MORRISON

DESERET
BOOK
SALT LAKE CITY, UTAH

Library of Congress Cataloging-in-Publication Data

Morrison, Alexander B.

    Valley of sorrow: a layman's guide to understanding mental illness / Alexander B. Morrison.
        p.   cm.
    Includes bibliographical references and index.
    ISBN 1-59038-087-8 (pbk. : alk. paper)
    1. Mental illness—Popular works.   2. Mental illness—Religious aspects—Mormon Church.   I. Title.
RC460.M668 2003
616.89—dc21   2003000512

Printed in the United States of America   54459-7109
Malloy Lithographing Incorporated
Ann Arbor, MI

10   9   8   7   6   5   4   3   2   1

For our beloved daughter Mary, whose faith, courage,
and insight inspire all who know her

CONTENTS

PREFACE ix

INTRODUCTION xi

CHAPTER 1   THE ENIGMA OF SUFFERING 1

CHAPTER 2   MYTHS AND MISCONCEPTIONS 19

CHAPTER 3   ANXIETY DISORDERS:
            PARALYZED WITH FEAR 31

CHAPTER 4   THE BLACK DOG OF DEPRESSION 49

CHAPTER 5   SCHIZOPHRENIA: DEMONS
            OF DARKNESS 75

CHAPTER 6   EATING DISORDERS:
            STARVATION AMIDST PLENTY 83

CONTENTS

CHAPTER 7   THE DARK SPECTER OF SUICIDE 99

CHAPTER 8   NOT MY WILL, BUT THINE, BE DONE ... 115

FOR ADDITIONAL INFORMATION 135

BIBLIOGRAPHY 137

INDEX 141

PREFACE

This book is not an official publication of The Church of
Jesus Christ of Latter-day Saints. No one asked me to
write it, and I alone am responsible for errors or omissions in
the text. The views and ideas presented herein are my own and
do not necessarily represent the position or view of the Church.

I am indebted to Gregory W. Ellis, M.D., for his great
clinical skills and caring, compassionate heart. Dr. Ellis read
each chapter carefully and made valuable suggestions for cor-
rections and additions to the manuscript. I am grateful also to
Fred Riley and Dr. Brent Scharman of LDS Family Services,
who provided valuable background information, read the
entire manuscript, and suggested ways to improve my draft
material.

I acknowledge with deep gratitude Shirley E. Morrison,
dear wife and mother, whose loving care and wise counsel
inspire all who know her. Her support for my attempt to write
this book has been unwavering.

Afton Ferris typed, proofread, and corrected the manuscript with great skill, going more than the extra mile in doing so.

This book is dedicated to our darling daughter Mary, whose courage, wisdom, insight, and devotion to the Savior stand as a shining example to all who know her. Her suffering, over many years, has refined and polished her character, and leaves us all in awe of her strength. She has been both the inspiration and the chief consultant for this book.

INTRODUCTION

In the Book of Mormon (2 Nephi 5:27) we read that the Nephites, who had, at least in the aggregate, been obedient to God's laws, "lived after the manner of happiness." What a wonderful and blessed state. And what a hopeful assurance: if we are obedient, and follow God's commandments, we can be happy, regardless of our circumstances. It sounds like a description of a cause-and-effect relationship, and so it is, or can be. There is plenty of evidence in the medical literature that amidst all of the problems of life, faithful, believing, and behaving Latter-day Saints live, in general, happier and more productive lives than those who squander their time and talents in hedonistic self-gratification. It is important to understand, however, that happiness does not necessarily require the absence of adversity. Indeed, it would be unwise and unrealistic to think that one can go through life without facing trials and tribulations. Every family—indeed, every individual—experiences temptation, opposition, suffering, and difficult trials that test faith and endurance. One of the great purposes of mortality is to prove our worthiness to receive the choicest blessings of our Heavenly Father through faithful endurance to the end, amidst all of the afflictions and sorrows life may bring to us. No mistake about it, adversity is part of God's plan for His children: "For it must needs be, that there is an opposition in all things" (2 Nephi 2:11).

Among the most painful—and often protracted—trials an individual or family can face is that of mental illness. By mental illness I do not mean the temporary, transient social and emotional concerns experienced as part of the normal wear and tear of living. Included in that category would be the temporary depression associated with the death of a friend or the anxiety felt when starting a new job. Nor do I include in the category of mental illness secondary effects of serious physical disorders, such as brain cancer or meningitis. By mental illness I mean a brain disorder that causes mild to severe disturbances in thinking, feeling, perception, and behavior. If such disturbances are sufficiently severe, and of sufficient duration, they may significantly impair a person's ability to cope with life's ordinary demands and routines. They may even threaten life itself—as in severe depression—or be so debilitating that the sufferer is unable to function effectively as an individual or productive member of society.

Specialists in the field of mental illness list a number of general categories of mental illness, including *anxiety disorders* (phobias, panic disorder, and obsessive-compulsive disorder); *mood disorders* (clinical depression and bipolar disorder); *schizophrenia* (a serious disorder that produces hallucinations, delusions, social withdrawal, and impaired reasoning); *dementias* (a group of disorders, including Alzheimer's disease, which lead to declines in mental functions, including loss of memory and of intellectual skills); and *eating disorders* (anorexia nervosa and bulimia, both serious and potentially life-threatening disorders). In this book I will deal, albeit superficially, with some of the most common mental illnesses but will not address others that, though painful and trying to all concerned, afflict relatively small numbers of persons.

As one would expect, there is a continuum between *social* and *emotional concerns* and *mental illnesses.* Emotional concerns are transient and result (presumably) from the ordinary stresses and strains of life. Many mental illnesses are believed to have biological factors that contribute to their causation, including chemical imbalances in the brain. A case in point: temporary sadness—such as occurs while grieving the loss of a friend—lies on one end of a continuum, and deep, continuous feelings of utter hopelessness and despair, leading perhaps to suicide, lie on the other. Indeed, about 15 percent of severely depressed patients kill themselves.

Though medical science has made marvelous progress in the last century in solving some of the mysteries of the brain, the simple truth is that knowledge in this vital and immensely complex area is still in its infancy. Although generally accepted hypotheses are beginning to emerge, we still do not know exactly how the brain works, nor exactly how and why parts of it may malfunction. One thing is certain, however: mental illness touches us all. More than one in five Americans experiences mental illness in a given year, and one in four Americans has a family member with a mental illness. No individual, family, or group is immune.

Of course, not all who are afflicted get help from therapists, ecclesiastical leaders, or, when needed, medication. Many just suffer, often unnecessarily, or muddle through as best they can on their own resources. Fortunately, we are learning that many mental illnesses result, in ways not yet totally understood, from the genetics of the cells of the brain, which influences how those cells function and communicate. Interaction between brain cells is mediated through chemical substances called neurotransmitters produced by the cells themselves. Genetic influences within the cell, often in conjunction with external factors, such as the lifestyle of the person involved, stress, dietary habits, use of psychoactive drugs, etc., may result in disturbed or abnormal functioning of the brain or portions thereof. Mental illness can result.

The analogy with other illnesses, such as diabetes, which results from a chemical disorder in the cells of the pancreas, is obvious. Advancement of knowledge in this immensely complex area has led to the development of a new science, pharmacogenetics—the science of generating medications to influence the brain cells at the level of their inner genetic makeup. In sum, therefore, the effective treatment of many mental disorders lies (in part) in the wise use of biological measures, just as treatment of high blood pressure may include the use of medication along with dietary and lifestyle changes.

Some who read this book may feel I have placed too much emphasis on the biological/medical model of mental illness. It is true that my training and orientation perhaps predispose me to that kind of approach. It is well to keep in mind, however, that mental illness cannot now and perhaps never will be fully explained on the basis of what we now know about biology. Mankind is both spirit and body (see D&C 88:115), and we are much more than just the sum of our physiology and anatomy. Mental illness is not just a matter of neuro-transmitters, genetic predisposition to changes in brain chemistry, and all the marvelous intricacies of neurobiology. It also involves inner conflicts, psychic pain, emotions, and feelings. "Talk therapy," in which the patient begins to understand why he or she thinks and acts in certain ways and learns effective coping behavior, in order not just to avoid psychic pain but to overcome it, remains of vital importance in dealing effectively with mental illness.

That said, however, we should not underestimate the effectiveness of medication, which has helped untold millions of those with mental illness to come back to reality, overcome despair, regain hope, quell their inner demons, and live useful and productive lives. It seems to me that we are not dealing with a black-and-white situation, despite the debates about medication versus psychotherapy that continue to swirl and eddy throughout the community of mental health professionals. It seems obvious that both medication and psychotherapy have invaluable roles to play. How the two are used, and in which "mix," will depend, of course, on the needs of the particular patient involved and the orientation and training of the caregiver. Both sets of disciplines fill essential roles. Ongoing research in both broad aspects of therapy is essential.

There is, indeed, evidence that at the most fundamental level, medication and psychotherapy act in a common way, by altering brain chemistry. Researchers at the UCLA School of Medicine, using positron emission tomography (PET) scanning techniques, have shown that cognitive-behavioral therapy alone, without medication, actually causes chemical changes in the brains of people with obsessive-compulsive disorder (OCD) (Jeffrey M. Schwartz, M.D., *Brain Lock*). Those changes can be induced through behavior therapy alone, or behavior therapy in combination with medication. The more behavior therapy is used, the less medication is needed.

In a recently published, important book, Dr. Jeffrey Schwartz has noted the emerging understanding that the brain has remarkable neuroplasticity—that it can in effect be "rewired," not just in childhood but throughout life. Adult patients can use their minds to reshape the function of their brains. Patients with depression, for example, can learn to process their emotions in new ways that do not trigger the thoughts and mood states characteristic of a depressive episode.

Schwartz's work, along with that of others, is providing scientific evidence for the existence of human free will, and hence of man's inherent capacity to make moral choices. We are not the captives of our neurons! (See Schwartz and Begley, *The Mind and the Brain*).

The community of professional caregivers in the mental health field, generally speaking, is divided between psychiatrists and psychotherapists—i.e., psychologists, social workers, and other licensed mental health professionals. Psychiatrists are medical doctors with specialized training in psychiatry and neurology. They also are trained to provide psychotherapy, though some psychologists would say some of them do so relatively less often and with less intensity and effectiveness than is desirable. Psychiatrists can, however, do some things psychologists cannot. They can prescribe medication and, since they are trained physicians, can determine if the patient is suffering from some other medical problem, such as a brain tumor, which could cause symptoms of mental illness.

Psychologists are trained, often at the doctoral level, to provide cognitive and behavioral therapy aimed at helping people with mental illness to understand why they feel and act as they do, and to assist them in developing behaviors that will aid in their healing. Many are excellent psychotherapists, as are psychiatric social workers and other trained mental health professionals.

Why is there still such misunderstanding and fear surrounding mental illness? Why do silence, ignorance, alienation, and prejudice concerning mental illness continue to abound? Why does mental illness carry such a powerful social stigma? Why is it so hard for so many to give up outdated and downright wrong ideas about mental illness and see it for what it really is—the mental "equivalent" of physical disorders?

I firmly believe that the only way to change public attitudes about mental illness is to bring light where there is darkness, knowledge where there is ignorance, and reason where there is superstition. That is, in fact, why I have written this book. I hope that after reading it, people will recognize that mental illness, in its many forms, qualitatively has much in common with physical illnesses, such as diabetes, heart disease, or arthritis. Diseases vary in cause and treatment, of course, but in each instance, a disorder of function in one or more of the organs of the body is involved. No matter what the disorder, whether physical or mental in origin, relief is to be found in an amalgam of remedies. Early diagnosis, help from ecclesiastical leaders, treatment by qualified health professionals, and appropriate effort on the part of the victim are required prerequisites for improvement.

This is not a clinical textbook; I was trained as a scientist, not as a physician or a clinical psychologist. Furthermore, although I make mention of at least some of the science involved, my intention is not to provide a text on psycho-pharmacology, pharmacogenetics, or neurophysiology. My intentions in writing this book are neither clinical nor scientific in nature. They go beyond signs and symptoms, diagnosis and treatment, to my wish to apply a healing balm of Gilead to the scarified, suffering souls afflicted with mental illness and to those who love them. My desire is to ease their burdens and lighten the loads that gall and weaken them; to help them to reach toward God and have hope and faith in Him and His purposes.

Above all else, my greatest hope is that this book, by providing information that replaces ignorance and misconceptions with truth, will bring a measure of hope and encouragement to those who suffer the terrible burdens of mental illness. I pray they may bear their afflictions with hope for the future and with the knowledge that God has not abandoned them. His love, I know, is ever present and never failing. As the Lord said to Moses, who marveled at the bush that burned with flame and yet was not consumed, "I have surely seen the affliction of my people . . . for I know their sorrows" (Exodus 3:6). God does indeed know our sorrows, for He "is mindful of every people, whatsoever land they may be in; yea, he numbereth his people, and his bowels of mercy are over all the earth" (Alma 26:37). There will be times when the love of God is all that sustains those who bear the heavy burden of affliction and languish in the dark pit of despair. But I know from experience that His love never fails. It will see us through, though we walk in the valley of the shadow of death itself (see Psalm 23).

I believe that in important ways those who suffer from mental illness—and that includes both the victims and those around them—can benefit from the experience of the great prophet Moses. Upon leaving Pharaoh's court, he was compelled to flee out of Egypt, across the desert to Midian (see Exodus 2:15). Eventually he came to a well and was refreshed by its life-giving water. By no means was his life's journey complete. Indeed, it is safe to say that it had just begun. Many sorrows and trials and much affliction awaited Moses in the future. But as he grew to know God and to understand that He is ever with us—perhaps especially in the seasons of our afflictions, even at times when we do not have the strength to call upon Him—Moses grew in his ability both to endure hardship and to look with hope to the future. So too can those who suffer from mental illness.

No small part of the suffering experienced by those with mental illness is the direct result of the ignorance, prejudice, and wrong-headed thinking of family members, friends, business associates, Church members, and others. I firmly believe that as in other areas of life, conveying the truth is the key to banishing the ignorance, stigma, and prejudice that surround mental illness. Such truth will, I trust, encourage sufferers from mental disorders to seek appropriate ecclesiastical and professional assistance, and help dispel their own debilitating fears, feelings of guilt, and self-doubt.

I am convinced that the best way to help those who suffer from mental illness is to express genuine love and interest, reassure the victim of God's perfect love, show unfailing compassion, listen more effectively, learn about the full nature of the illness, withhold judgment, and provide needed help. As we try to help, we must ever remember that the circle of suffering usually extends beyond the primary victim to include spouse, other family members, associates, and friends. All who are involved need sincere love, compassion, and understanding. As John Winthrop, later the first governor of Massachusetts, said to fellow Puritans aboard the *Arabella* on their voyage to what has evolved into the United States of America: "We must be knit together in this work as one. . . . We must delight in each other; make other's conditions our own; rejoice together, mourn together, labor and suffer together . . . as members of the same body" (Robert C. Winthrop, *Life and Letters of John Winthrop,* 18–19).

Chapter One

THE ENIGMA
OF SUFFERING

Mental illness, in its various causes, forms, and manifestations, ranks high on any list of the ailments that try and torment mankind. In its publication *The Global Burden of Disease,* the World Health Organization (WHO) estimated, for example, that one form of mental illness, depression, was the fourth most important reported health problem in the developing world in 1990. The WHO predicts that by 2020, depression may rank as the number one health problem in that portion of the globe. If we add to the enormous burdens resulting from depression those that flow from all other types and manifestations of mental illness in both the developed and developing worlds, it is clear that these disorders have an enormous effect on victims, their families, friends, and associates and on society in general.

One of the greatest burdens created by mental illnesses is the pain and suffering they cause. These effects are almost indescribable. One author has pointed out, for example, that "the pain of severe depression is quite unimaginable to those who have not suffered it, and it kills in many instances because its anguish can no longer be borne" (William Styron, *Darkness Visible*, 33). Victims of severe depression often tell of a terrible black cloud of despair and darkness that envelops them—a "malignant sadness," as Lewis Wolpert describes the depression that he barely survived (*Malignant Sadness: The Anatomy of Depression*). Afflicted persons may cry all day and be unable to work, to think, or even to get out of bed. In their agony, they may abuse alcohol or other drugs, or even commit suicide (as in fact one in six sufferers from severe depression does).

Those afflicted with panic attacks or other anxiety disorders also suffer horrendously. They describe their ordeal "as though a thousand pound weight were pressing on my chest," as though "I'm slowly suffocating in darkness," so "frightened I'm simply paralyzed," or "I think I will die at any moment." Their world shrinks as they withdraw in hopes they can avoid triggering a cataclysm of pain and panic.

Sufferers from another relatively common mental illness called obsessive-compulsive disorder (OCD) may exhibit obsessive behavior, characterized by repetitive senseless thoughts, which the victim cannot stop ruminating about. For example, he or she may be plagued by repetitive thoughts or images of death and imagine in gruesome detail car wrecks or plane crashes. Victims of OCD also may exhibit compulsive behavior, characterized by unnecessary repetitive acts. For example, they may wash their hands over and over again, dozens of times a day; or check dozens of times, one after the other, to ensure the doors are locked in the house; or go through an elaborate, fixed, unchangeable ritual in making a bed, preparing a meal, or even in sitting down.

Psychotic symptoms, in which the patient breaks with reality, are common to several mental illnesses, including schizophrenia and the manic phase of bipolar depression. Psychotic patients may hear voices when no one is talking or, less commonly, experience visual hallucinations, seeing things that are not there. Psychotic symptoms occurring in schizophrenia, or as part of depression, usually involve hearing voices that tell the victim he or she is a terrible human being who deserves to die or has done horrible things requiring punishment, or voices that direct the afflicted person to commit some heinous act.

These frightening symptoms—and I have by no means mentioned the whole catalog of those found in psychiatric illnesses—are immensely terrifying to victims and to family members and friends who vicariously share in their pain and fear. The problem is magnified by the social stigma associated with having a mental illness or seeking treatment for it. Persons who believe they or someone they love is in need of competent medical or psychological assistance for a mental disorder fear, with good reason, they will be ridiculed and shunned if they seek such help. They fear their spouse, children, friends, or employer will abandon them or that no one will have them in marriage. Career opportunities are decreased significantly, and health insurance companies commonly limit their coverage of psychiatric care. They may even refuse to insure those with mental illness. How ironic it is that one can qualify for financial reimbursement for the treatment of a mild disorder such as an ingrown toenail, but not for the treatment of a life-threatening disorder such as severe depression!

The social stigmatization of sufferers from mental disorders is no small thing. For example, a candidate for the vice-presidency of the United States, Thomas Eagleton, U. S. Senator from Missouri, was forced to withdraw from the national political campaign in 1972 when it was revealed in the national media that he had received electroconvulsive shock treatment for depression.

But the problem is even worse. Many mentally ill persons blame themselves for their condition. This is especially common in the early stages of their illness, when insight has not yet had time to grow and develop. They feel ashamed of themselves for being sick. They think of themselves as weak and spineless. They torture themselves with recurring thoughts that somehow, in some way, they know not how, they have sinned and are being punished by God. Widespread, long-held public attitudes that attribute mental illness to divine punishment only increase the problem. Latter-day Saints are particularly vulnerable to these false beliefs. In the Book of Mormon we are informed that "wickedness never was happiness" (Alma 41:10). It is all too easy to twist that doctrinal truth a fraction, however unknowingly, into a belief that unhappiness is always due to wickedness. All too often it is assumed by uninformed people that those who are suffering from mental illness are somehow responsible for their plight, that they have brought it upon themselves by sinful behavior.

The Prophet Joseph Smith understood that not all suffering is caused by sin.

> It is a false idea that the Saints will escape all the judgments, whilst the wicked suffer; for all flesh is subject to suffer, and 'the righteous shall hardly escape' [see D&C 63:34]; still many of the Saints will escape, for the just shall live by faith; yet many of the righteous shall fall a prey to disease, to

pestilence, etc., by reason of the weakness of the flesh, and yet be saved in the Kingdom of God. So that it is an unhallowed principle to say that such and such have transgressed because they have been preyed upon by disease or death, for all flesh is subject to death; and the Savior has said, 'Judge not, lest ye be judged'" [see Matthew 7:1] (*History of the Church,* 4:11).

Parents and spouses commonly blame themselves, both for the cause of their loved one's illness and for their inability to bring relief, even healing, to the one who is affected. "If only I were a better mother, she wouldn't have gotten sick," or "If I were only a more righteous man, God would hear and answer my prayers," they may say. The latter can be a particularly harrowing agony for men who bear the holy priesthood and know that priesthood power can bless and heal the afflicted. "What kind of priesthood bearer am I," they may cry, "if I can't even bless the life of my beloved daughter?"

In their agony of spirit, persons with mental illness commonly ask why it is they have to suffer so much. They may pray over and over again, day in and day out, for relief that does not come. They may know of others who have been healed and may have heard accounts of miraculous interventions and recovery. In their grief and confusion they may become bitter and angry. They may feel deserted by God and deprived of His love, and may long to die. Thus spake Job when he, for good reason, undoubtedly was depressed: "Let the day perish wherein I was born, and the night in which it was said, There is a man child conceived. . . . Why died I not from the womb? . . . Wherefore is light given to him that is in misery, and life unto the bitter in soul; which long for death, but it cometh not; and dig for it more than for hid treasures;

which rejoice exceedingly, and are glad, when they can find the grave?" (Job 3:3, 11, 20–22).

Do not judge Job too harshly. Given the enormity of his suffering, we ought to readily understand the anguish of his soul and empathize with him. Even the Prophet Joseph Smith, having been imprisoned without cause and treated inhumanely by brutal guards for weeks on end, cried out in agony and despair: "O God, where art thou? And where is the pavilion that covereth thy hiding place? How long shall thy hand be stayed, and thine eye, yea thy pure eye, behold from the eternal heavens the wrongs of thy people and of thy servants, and thine ear be penetrated with their cries?" (D&C 121:1–2). To His sorrowing son came the Father's gentle reply: "My son, peace be unto thy soul; thine adversity and thine afflictions shall be but a small moment; and then, if thou endure it well, God shall exalt thee on high; thou shalt triumph over all thy foes. . . . Thou art not yet as Job; thy friends do not contend against thee, neither charge thee with transgression, as they did Job" (D&C 121:7–8,10).

From time immemorial mankind has tried to make sense of suffering. We ask, why do the righteous suffer while some of the ungodly apparently get off scot-free? Why is there such an unfair distribution of suffering in the world? In a world where God's justice and mercy reign, why do we read every day of senseless murders, of innocent children abused by wicked adults, of terrorist attacks on helpless bystanders, of the horror of "ethnic cleansing" in response to ancient tribal hatreds? Or, closer to home, how do we explain the tragedy of a young teenager struck down and killed by a careless joyrider, or of a whole family wiped out by a drunken driver, while on the way home from a family wedding? Or, why are even our young missionaries sometimes killed while in the service of the Lord? Why, why, why do such things happen? And, perhaps most poignantly, why is this pain and sorrow happening to me? I live righteously and have done all the Lord asks, and yet He still allows this illness to remain.

To try to understand why so many bad things happen to good people, we must first wrestle with the causation of suffering. In doing so, it would be well to admit at the outset that "the Lord seeth not as man seeth" (1 Samuel 16:7). Mortal views are at best myopic and incomplete. *We do not see the beginning from the end, as God does.* As Elder Neal A. Maxwell has wisely said, "We cannot do the sums because we do not have all the numbers" (*All These Things Shall Give Thee Experience,* 37). We simply lack an eternal perspective.

In order to even partially understand the causes of suffering, we need to know the following:

GOD OUR FATHER IS OMNISCIENT

Jacob, the faithful younger brother of Nephi, understood that God is all-knowing, all-powerful, ever-present: "O how great the holiness of our God! For he knoweth all things, and there is not anything save he knows it" (2 Nephi 9:20). In the *Lectures on Faith,* prepared by the Prophet Joseph Smith and others, and personally approved by the Prophet himself, we read, "God is the only supreme governor and independent being in whom all fullness and perfection dwell; who is omnipotent, omnipresent, and omniscient; without beginning of days or end of life; and . . . in him every good gift and every good principle dwell" (*Lectures on Faith* (1985), 10). In a letter of 1834 to the Saints who had been scattered from their homes in Missouri, the Presidency of the High Priesthood (in effect, the First Presidency) gave further insight on the omniscience of God: "We admit that God is the great source and fountain from whence proceeds all good; that He is perfect intelligence, and that His wisdom is alone sufficient to govern and regulate the mighty creations and worlds which shine and blaze with such magnificence and splendor over our heads, as though touched with His finger and moved by His Almighty word" (*History of the Church*, 2:12).

Note that there are no qualifiers in the scriptures or the words of the living prophets concerning the omniscience of God, whose "understanding is infinite" (Psalm 147:5), and who "knoweth all things which are to come" (Words of Mormon 1:7). He who knows the end from the beginning knows all that is in between. We, who can teach Him nothing, can have *absolute* faith in His *absolute* knowledge! Thus, He knows, in infinite detail, the trials that await *each* of His children, as He knows too our ability to withstand them and grow spiritually from them.

God does not need the learning opportunities that come to us in mortality. His work and glory come not from learning new facts nor from constantly revising, expanding, and remodeling His knowledge, but from the increase and advancement of His creations, bringing to flower and fruition the immortality and eternal life of His children. There are no aspects of reality that stand independent of His foreknowledge and divine will. On this point I regretfully part company with Rabbi Harold S. Kushner, who argues that there still remains residual chaos in the world, that the process of replacing chaos with order is still going on in the universe, that events occur outside of the laws of nature, and that God therefore is unable to influence all human affairs (see chapter 3, *When Bad Things Happen to Good People*). Such thinking, sincere though it is, I believe to be incompatible with the reality of God's omniscience and omnipotence.

God's eternal progression, then, does not lie in His attainment of additional knowledge. President Joseph Fielding Smith enunciated that principle well when he observed that God's progression occurs "not by seeking knowledge which he does not have, for such a thought cannot be maintained in the light of scripture. It is not through ignorance and learning hidden truth that he progresses, for if there are truths which he does not know, then these things are greater than he, and this cannot be" (*Selections from Doctrines of Salvation*, 6).

We must look elsewhere than in the nature and character of God for the causation of suffering.

TIME IS A HUMAN CHALLENGE

With God, the past, present, and future are part of an "eternal now." As the Prophet Joseph Smith explained, "The great Jehovah contemplated the whole of the events connected with the earth, pertaining to the plan of salvation, before it rolled into existence, or ever 'the morning stars sang together' for joy; . . . He [is] acquainted with the situation of all nations and with their destiny; He [orders] all things according to the council of His own will; He knows the situation of both the living and the dead, and has made ample provision for their redemption, according to their several circumstances, and the laws of the kingdom of God, whether in this world, or in the world to come" (*History of the Church*, 4:597). Truly, as the psalmist sang of God: "For a thousand years in thy sight are but as yesterday when it is past, and as a watch in the night" (Psalm 90:4).

We mortals, on the other hand, are bound in our earthly existence by the confines of time, by the rising and the setting of the sun, the rhythms of the seasons, birth and death, the ticking of the clock, the inevitability of tomorrow's deadline. Yet even so, we are always uneasy, never really at home in time. We have intimations of immortality: we glimpse, as through a glass, darkly (see 1 Corinthians 13:12), a world before we came to this earth, and life beyond mortality. We belong to eternity; we are eternal beings; our essence, that which is at our very core, is without beginning of days or end of years. Time is not our natural dimension, and eventually its constraints will be lifted from us (see D&C 84:100).

What does all this have to do with suffering? Simply this: that which we think is interminable, everlasting, forever, is in God's eyes but a moment—barely the fluttering of an eyelid in an eternal journey. Someday—and it will be soon for all of us, in God's reckoning—the veil between mortality and eternity will be parted, and we will see forever. Then—if not before—we will realize that our trials and tribulations of today, sore and vexing though they are or may be, are no more. And we will recognize the truth of what God said to the Prophet Joseph Smith: "All these things shall give thee experience, and shall be for thy good" (D&C 122:7).

The Father's Great Plan of Happiness Requires That We Be Tried and Tested

When the formation of the earth was being discussed in the great council in heaven, Jesus Christ, who stood among those in attendance as one who "was like unto God," proclaimed: "We will go down, for there is space there, and we will take of these materials, and we will make an earth whereon these [i.e., the spirit children of God] may dwell; and we will prove them herewith, to see if they will do all things whatsoever the Lord their God shall command them" (Abraham 3:24–25). Our mortal experience, our "second estate," thus is a time when we will be tested and tried. Mortality is a time for learning, even though that effort may be nearly more than we can bear—confusing, well-nigh inexplicable, soul-wrenching. C. S. Lewis spoke of how God remodels us, if we will but let Him, sometimes in ways that hurt and don't seem, on the surface, to make sense:

"Imagine yourself as a living house. God comes in to rebuild that house. At first, perhaps, you can understand what He is doing. He is getting the drains right and stopping the leaks in the roof and so on: you knew that those jobs needed doing and so you are not surprised. But presently he starts knocking the house about in a way that hurts abominably and does not seem to make sense. What on earth is He up to? The explanation is that He is building quite a different house from the one you thought of—throwing out a new wing here, putting on an extra floor there, running up towers, making courtyards. You thought you were going to be made into a decent little cottage: but He is building a palace" (*Mere Christianity*, 172).

At times, in God's remodeling of our lives, it is required that we go to the outer limits of our faith, when all we can do is hang on, trusting that He knows what is best for us, even when we feel bruised and battered by life. We may be surprised, even confused at what is happening, but He is not. God, the Omniscient One, who comprehends all things past, present, and future, knows full well how we will cope with adversity and tribulation. Though He knows us perfectly, and loves us completely, His foreknowledge does not impinge on our agency because, as we approach our trials, we are free to choose one course of action or another. Our decisions are made in the light of *our* knowledge, not *His*. We do not know what He knows. God takes our decisions into account so that His tutoring proceeds as it should, and His purposes—to help us grow spiritually and become more like Him—are not frustrated. Thus "we know that all things work together for good to them that love God" (Romans 8:28).

President Boyd K. Packer has spoken about the need for us to walk to the very edge of the light given to us, and beyond if necessary, confident that God will open the way for us. He said: "Shortly after I was called as a General Authority, I went to Elder Harold B. Lee for counsel. He listened very carefully to my problem and suggested that I see President David O. McKay. President McKay counseled me as to the direction I would go. I was very willing to be obedient but saw no way possible for me to do as he counseled me to do.

"I returned to Elder Lee and told him that I saw no way to move in the direction I was counseled to go. He said, 'The trouble with you is you want to see the end from the beginning.' I replied that I would like to see at least a step or two ahead. Then came the lesson of a lifetime: 'You must learn to walk to the edge of the light, and then a few steps into the darkness; then the light will appear and show the way before you'" ("The Edge of the Light," 22–23).

The Father's great plan of happiness, known also by other terms, including the plan of salvation (see Alma 42:5), teaches us that mankind *chose* to enter mortality; that we came to earth with full understanding that to do so would inevitably require us to suffer. President Spencer W. Kimball wrote:

"We knew before we were born that we were coming to the earth for bodies and experience and that we would have joys and sorrows, ease and pain, comforts and hardships, health and sickness, successes and disappointments. We knew also that after a period of life we would die. We accepted all these eventualities with a glad heart, eager to accept both the favorable and the unfavorable. We eagerly accepted the chance to come earthward even though it might be for only a day or a year. Perhaps we were not so much concerned whether we should die of disease, of accident, or of senility. We were willing to take life as it came and as we might organize and control it, and this without murmur, complaint, or unreasonable demands."

President Kimball also noted: "We sometimes think we would like to know what was ahead, but sober thought brings us back to accepting life a day at a time and magnifying and glorifying that day" (*Tragedy or Destiny,* 12, 11).

It is apparent that suffering is inherent in mortality. Only in the hereafter, in the glory of God's presence, will the full effect of Christ's atonement be felt. Then, "God shall wipe away all tears from their eyes; and there shall be no more death, neither sorrow, nor crying, neither shall there be any more pain" (Revelation 21:4).

Against this brief background, what can we say about the cause of suffering? It is apparent suffering can result from several causes. They include the following:

1. Suffering may result from our own folly, foolishness, or wickedness.

In such instances—and they are legion, given the propensity of human beings to err—we have only ourselves to blame. If we sow the wind, we will reap the whirlwind. It is the law of the harvest in action, as Paul wrote to the Galatian Saints (see Galatians 6).

2. We may suffer because of the sins of others.

"Man's inhumanity to man," the poet Robert Burns said, "makes countless thousands mourn" (*The Oxford Dictionary of Quotations,* 114). Beginning with Cain's murder of his brother, the long, lamentable litany of human crime provides eloquent witness to the suffering borne by the innocent at the hands of the wicked.

3. We may suffer because we are Christians.

The Apostle Peter warned: "But let none of you suffer as a murderer, or as a thief, or as an evil-doer, or as a busybody in other men's matters. Yet if any man suffer as a Christian, let him not be ashamed; but let him glorify God on this behalf" (1 Peter 4:15–16). President Joseph F. Smith noted that there never have been a people united in the service of God as His covenant people who have not been "hated and persecuted by the wicked" (see *Gospel Doctrine*, 46).

4. We may suffer as an inevitable consequence of life itself.

We live in a world governed by natural laws, not all of which operate for our short-term benefit. Thus, we have no immunity against a host of diseases and cannot escape the accidents and misfortunes that are inherent in our own biology or are related to the physical world in which we live. If we fall by accident, we may break a bone, suffer a concussion, or even die. If we are infected by the influenza virus, we will probably get sick. As we get older we suffer the natural results of aging. Disease, accidents, death itself may be delayed, but ultimately cannot be avoided. Each is associated with suffering. It is all part of the natural order of things, one of the conditions we agreed to when we came to earth.

5. We may suffer as part of the Lord's testing and trying of us.

"For whom the Lord loveth he chasteneth, and scourgeth every son whom he receiveth" (Hebrews 12:6). God is willing to permit us to undergo trials and tribulations because He knows that our spiritual strength is directly related to the extent to which our souls are stretched. That is not to say we should therefore seek for suffering and glory in tribulation. Far from it. There is no intrinsic value in suffering. Latter-day Saints do not believe that mortification of the flesh—the wearing of a literal or figurative hair shirt—has anything to do in and of itself with the growth of our souls. Suffering can wound and embitter the soul, as surely as it can strengthen and purify. Some souls become stronger under suffering, but some break.

It all depends on our response. "I do not believe," said Anne Morrow Lindbergh, "that sheer suffering teaches. If suffering alone taught, all the world would be wise, since everyone suffers. To suffering must be added mourning, understanding, patience, love, openness, and the willingness to remain vulnerable" (*Time* magazine, Feb. 5, 1973, 35).

Though I recognize God is omnipotent, I do not believe He actually afflicts people with mental illness, or other ailments either. For example, I do not believe He stipulates that this person be depressed or that person schizophrenic. But in His omniscience, He knows a trial is coming to us and *declines to remove it,* using it as a tutoring tool, to help us to grow spiritually. He knows every detail of our DNA and hence of our genetic propensities to resist or acquire disease, including mental disorders. So too He knows fully all the myriad of biological, social, and environmental factors to which we will be exposed during our lifetimes, and He understands completely the effect they will have on us. He knows when genetic predisposition will converge with a stressful lifestyle or emotional trauma to produce disorder, perhaps even serious disease. Not all His children pass with flying colors the various tests to which they are subjected, but those who do so become stronger spiritually. Furthermore, while granting that God can do whatever He wishes, I do not believe for a moment He uses the suffering of mental illness to punish His children. No mistake about it: sin certainly *can* cause mental illness, but God is not the source either of the sin or the resultant affliction. I believe His very nature forbids it. The Prophet Joseph Smith wisely noted: "A man is his own tormentor and his own condemner. Hence the saying, They shall go down into the lake that burns with fire and brimstone. The torment of disappointment in the mind of man is as exquisite as a lake burning with fire and brimstone. I say, so is the torment of man" (*History of the Church,* 6:314).

That said, however, and fully recognizing that all mortals sin, in the sense that all fall short of perfection, the vast majority of the mentally ill are not sick because they are gross sinners. Furthermore, they are not sick because God is punishing them but because they have a disorder of body function, resulting from natural causes and treatable using the knowledge God has given to skilled health care providers. If we do not believe that people get osteoarthritis or tuberculosis because they are sinners, why would we accept that they get obsessive-compulsive disorder or schizophrenia because they are sinners? Such thinking just doesn't make sense.

In sum, therefore, mental illness causes intense suffering, both to its victims and to others around them. Though God does not cause mental illness, in the sense that He does not *make* us mentally ill, He may decline to remove the "thorn in the flesh" which afflicts us, and use the suffering involved to test and tutor us, so that our souls may grow as they are stretched by trial and adversity. Whether our suffering causes our souls to grow or to canker depends on our response.

One of the most difficult things to accept is the wintry realization that God has declined to remove an onerous and galling burden from your back and your heart, and you will have to tread the winepress alone (see Isaiah 63:3). Perhaps we have thought, in our lack of understanding, in our spiritual immaturity, that "[God] would give [an answer] unto [us], when [we] took no thought save it was to ask [Him]" (D&C 9:7).

When the pain goes on and on, and prayers are not answered as we had hoped—even expected—they would be, sufferers come to a great crisis of faith. Testimonies hang on the way in which they respond to that challenge.

Persons suffering from mental illness who have received a priesthood blessing and have prayed fervently for relief may feel caught between their faith and the need to reach out for professional help. It is not unknown for a severely depressed person who has received a priesthood blessing to stop taking medication in order to show God their faith in the blessing. Weeks later, deep in depression again, they fear to go back on their medication, thinking, wrongly, that to do so reveals a lack of faith. I believe it is important for people to understand that getting appropriate professional help is not contrary to the exercise of faith. In fact, exercising faith may require following the advice of health professionals. Acquiring spiritual maturity is the hardest of all labors, and can be immensely painful, particularly if the quest occurs in the face of the intense emotional distress associated with mental illness. It is only when the fear, confusion, disappointment, and even anger of the sufferer give way to acceptance and submission that peace finally can come. Then and only then do we truly understand the Savior's words: "Not my will, but thine, be done" (Luke 22:42). Time, many tears, and much prayer are required.

In presenting this viewpoint, I recognize there are many persistent myths and misperceptions concerning mental illness. Let us now turn to a discussion of some of the most prevalent wrong ideas in this vitally important field.

Chapter Two

MYTHS AND MISCONCEPTIONS

As many myths and misconceptions about the cause, course, and treatment of mental illness unfortunately are found among Latter-day Saints as they are in the general public. These harmful and destructive attitudes include the following:

1. All mental illness is caused by sin.

I reiterate what was already stated in chapter 1: sin—the deliberate breaking of God's commandments—does indeed result in much behavior that is hurtful to self and to others. To every transgression there must needs be—by reason of the law of the harvest—a consequent punishment. The demands of justice are inexorable, unless the person concerned invokes the power of the mercy provided by Christ's atonement, by repenting of the sin involved, forsaking it, and accepting Christ as his or her personal Savior.

The power of sin to torment and harrow up the soul is vividly described by the repentant Alma: "But I was racked with eternal torment, for my soul was harrowed up to the greatest degree and racked with all my sins. . . . I was tormented with the pains of hell; . . . the very thought of coming into the presence of my God did rack my soul with inexpressible horror. Oh, thought I, that I could be banished and become extinct both soul and body" (Alma 36:12–15).

Those, like Alma, who experience sorrow and feelings of remorse during the repentance process are not mentally ill. But they do require confession and counseling at the hands of their bishop. As part of his calling, each bishop receives special powers of discernment and wisdom. No mental health professional, regardless of his or her skill, can ever replace the role of the faithful bishop, as he is guided by the Holy Ghost, in assisting Church members to work through the pain, remorse, and depression associated with sin.

That being said and fully acknowledged, however, it must be reemphasized that in *many* instances aberrant thoughts, actions, and feelings result from mental illness and not from sin. They come, as I have said, from *mental illness,* not *transgression.* They are *not* God's way of punishing the sinner. To assume they are is not only simplistic but also contrary to the teachings of Christ's Church (see pages 4–5). The bishop's first task in this matter is to discern whether a deeply distressed member of his congregation is suffering the effects of sin or of mental illness. He is able to do so effectively as he understands the nature and symptoms of mental illness and is guided by the Holy Ghost in his questioning and counsel. With a little factual knowledge, *and* the guidance of the Spirit, the faithful bishop will know how best to assist those in his care who are having problems. If they are mentally ill, he will refer them to a health professional for treatment, with his blessing, advising them to remain faithful.

The truth is that *many* faithful Latter-day Saints, who live the commandments and honor their covenants, experience personal struggles with mental illness, or are required to deal, perhaps over long periods of time, with the intense pain and suffering of morally righteous mentally ill family members. Those involved often carry the resultant pain, anxiety, and burdens without loving acceptance or understanding from others. I assure you that Church leaders are in no way exempt from the burden of mental illness, whether as victim, caregiver, family member, or friend. In the geographic area of every ward and stake there are severely depressed men and women; elderly people with failing memories and reduced intellectual capacities; youth or adults struggling with substance abuse; persons of all ages, both sexes, and every walk of life, who exhibit aberrant, even bizarre behavior. Their burdens—and they are many and painful—can be lifted only by love, understanding (both intellectual and spiritual), nonjudgmental acceptance, and appropriate assistance.

Not long ago, for example, I met a man, a gifted physician in his mid-forties, who began about five years ago to exhibit the intense, excessive, and painful mood swings of bipolar disorder. His problem is *mental illness,* not *sin.* Fortunately, he now is receiving effective medical treatment for his malady.

Closely related to the idea that all mental illness is caused by sin is the equally false notion that if you're living as you should, you won't have problems. Life, for you, will be the proverbial "bowl of cherries": after all, "men are, that they might have joy" (2 Nephi 2:25), and if you're keeping the commandments you can reasonably expect to be joyful all the time. In fact, God owes it to you, or so you might think. But you would be wrong.

Life doesn't work that way. Were there no opposition, spiritual advancement would not be possible. If there were no opposition, "righteousness could not be brought to pass, neither wickedness, neither holiness nor misery, neither good nor bad. Wherefore, all things must needs be a compound in one; wherefore, if it should be one body it must needs remain as dead, having no life neither death, nor corruption nor incorruption, happiness nor misery, neither sense nor insensibility. Wherefore, it must needs have been created for a thing of naught; wherefore there would have been no purpose in the end of its creation. Wherefore, this thing must needs destroy the wisdom of God and his eternal purposes, and also the power, and the mercy, and the justice of God" (2 Nephi 2:11–12).

Without misery there can be no joy. Tragedy, sorrow, afflictions, all are part of living. And it is a blessing they are, though often we have difficulty in understanding why it is so. Through the grace of a loving Father in Heaven, whose very purpose is to bring His children back to Him, none of us is exempt from tears and sorrow. All of God's children can expect to experience them.

2. Someone is to blame for mental illness.

Closely related to the myth that mental illness is caused by sin is the equally dangerous misconception that someone is to blame for mental illness. It is, I suppose, a common human tendency to blame others, or oneself, for whatever goes wrong

22

in life. Many victims of mental illness wear themselves out emotionally by repetitive futile attempts to remember something they, their parents, or someone else *might* have done, sometime, somewhere, that resulted in the terrible suffering they are forced to endure. Some blame their problem on demonic possession. While there is no doubt that such has occurred in *very rare* instances, let us take care not to give the devil credit for everything that goes awry in the world! Generally speaking, the mentally ill do not need exorcism; they need instead love, care, understanding, and support from everyone else, including their ecclesiastical leaders, as well as appropriate therapy from a skilled health care provider.

Most often, lacking an understanding about the causes of mental illness, victims blame *themselves,* and many seem unable to rid themselves of terrible though undefined feelings that somehow, some way *they* are the cause of their own pain—even when they're not. Parents, spouses, or other family members of mentally ill persons too often needlessly harrow up their own minds, trying futilely to determine where *they* went wrong. They pray over and over again for forgiveness, when there is no objective evidence they have anything of note for which to be forgiven. They may try to bargain with God, offering Him anything, even their own lives, if only He will "cure" their beloved child or family member. Of course, in the vast majority of instances none of this works, for the simple reason that the victim's thoughts and behavior result from disease processes, which are not caused by the actions of others, including God.

Those who play the "blame game" with themselves, believing their mental illness is somehow their fault, almost inevitably end up harboring intense though unjustified feelings of guilt and shame. They may go to great lengths to conceal the taking of medication, visits to a therapist, and so on. "What if my bishop finds out?" cried a woman taking Prozac for her depression. She was frightened and full of guilt for what she considered, falsely, to be shameful or weak behavior. Somehow, she thought in her confusion, she must be lacking in faith. She had prayed often to be rid of her depression, and when her prayers weren't answered as she longed for, she became convinced that was evidence of divine disapproval of her and tangible proof she was without faith and merely receiving her just deserts.

A wise bishop would not, of course, consider that a person taking Prozac or any other drug prescribed by a doctor for mental illness is any more likely to be guilty of wrongdoing or shameful behavior than if he or she were taking insulin for diabetes. Having determined, with the aid of the Spirit, that the person involved is suffering from mental illness and not the effects of sin, the bishop should encourage the member to continue to pray; attend appropriate meetings; participate in sacred ordinances; fulfill all other religious obligations; *and* get appropriate professional help—either from a physician or a skilled psychotherapist.

Ascribing blame for mental illness causes unnecessary suffering for all concerned and takes time and energy that would better be used in other ways: seeking to obtain a complete assessment and proper diagnosis of the illness involved, understanding its causes, learning behavioral and cognitive techniques that are part of the healing process, and obtaining proper medication that will help control the disorder by reversing the resultant chemical changes. As victims, loved ones, and all the rest of us come to understand mental illness more clearly, patience, forgiveness, and empathy will replace denial, anger, and rejection.

3. All that people with mental illness need is a priesthood blessing.

I am a great advocate and supporter of priesthood blessings. I know, from many personal experiences, that they do inestimable good. I know too that final and complete healing in mental illness or any other disease comes from faith in Jesus Christ. In any and all circumstances, in sickness and in health, in good times and bad, our lives will improve and become richer and more peaceful as we turn to Him. "Come unto me, all ye that labour and are heavy laden," He said. "Take my yoke upon you, and learn of me; for I am meek and lowly in heart: and ye shall find rest unto your souls. For my yoke is easy, and my burden is light" (Matthew 11:28–30). He and only He has ownership of the healing "balm of Gilead" needed by all of God's children.

However, without in any way denigrating the unique role of priesthood blessings, may I suggest that ecclesiastical leaders are spiritual leaders and should not be expected to take on the roles of mental health professionals. Almost all of them lack the professional skills and training to deal effectively with deep-seated mental illnesses and are well advised to seek competent professional assistance for those in their charge who are in need. Remember that God has given us wondrous knowledge and technology that can help us overcome grievous problems such as mental illness. Just as we would not hesitate to consult a physician about medical problems such as cancer, heart disease, or diabetes, so too we should not hesitate to obtain medical and other appropriate professional assistance in dealing with mental illness. When such assistance is sought, we must be careful to ensure, insofar as possible, that the health professional concerned follows practices and procedures that are compatible with gospel principles.

4. Mentally ill persons just lack willpower.

Some there are who, in their lack of understanding and empathy, mistakenly believe that the mentally ill just need to "snap out of it," "show a little backbone," and "straighten up!" These insensitive souls subscribe to what others have called "the Sock School of Psychiatry"—just pull them up and get on with it! Unfortunately, such bravado just doesn't work. Those who prescribe such an approach display a grievous lack of knowledge and compassion. The facts are that seriously mentally ill persons simply *cannot*, through an exercise of will, get out of the predicament they are in. They need help, encouragement, understanding, and love. Anyone who has ever witnessed the incredible, well-nigh unbearable pain of a severe panic attack knows full well that *nobody* would suffer that way if all that was needed was to show a little willpower. No one who has witnessed the almost indescribable sadness of a severely depressed person, who perhaps can't even get out of bed, who cries all day, retreats into hopeless apathy, or tries to kill himself, would ever think for a moment that mental illness is just a problem of willpower. No one who has witnessed the bizarre delusions and frightening hallucinations of a schizophrenic would ever think that a little willpower is all that is needed to restore that person to health. We don't say to persons with heart disease or cancer, "Oh, just grow up and get over it." Neither should we treat the mentally ill in such uncompassionate and unhelpful ways.

None of this should be taken to suggest in any way that all persons with mental illness are helpless victims, unable to do anything to help themselves. In many, many instances, sufferers can do something to help themselves and must be encouraged to do so.

5. Mentally ill persons are dangerous and should be locked up.

Sensational and grossly inaccurate and incomplete media reports have conjured up stereotypical portrayals of the mentally ill as crazed and violent lunatics, dangerous to others as well as themselves. The truth is that the vast majority of people with mental illness are *not* violent. The great majority of crimes of violence are *not* committed by persons who are mentally ill, in any generally acceptable sense of the term. In the relatively few instances where mentally ill people do become violent, the incident typically results from the same causes as with the general public, such as feelings of being threatened or the effects of drugs or alcohol or both.

Furthermore, over the last forty years, as effective medications for mental illness have become available and successful programs of behavioral and cognitive therapy have been developed, it has been shown that most mentally ill people—like those with physical illnesses—can live productive lives in their communities. They do not need to be "locked up." Like everyone else, mentally ill persons who are receiving proper treatment have the potential to work at any level in any trade or profession, depending solely on their abilities, talents, experience, and motivation. I need hardly mention, for example, Mike Wallace of the CBS television program "60 Minutes," who has had several bouts of severe depression but with appropriate treatment has gone on to live an accomplished life as a distinguished journalist. Similarly, Tipper Gore, the wife of former Vice President Al Gore, has successfully struggled with depression and has courageously chosen to discuss her problems publicly.

6. Mental illness doesn't strike children and young people.

As noted by the National Mental Health Association ("Stigma: Building Awareness and Understanding"), the truth is that an estimated six million young people in America suffer from a mental health disorder that severely disrupts their functioning at home, in school, or in the community. The majority of children who kill themselves are profoundly depressed, and most parents did not recognize that depression until it was too late. I reiterate: no one is immune from mental illness.

7. Whatever the cause, mental illness is untreatable.

As mentioned, during the past forty years numerous medications, effective against one or more forms of mental illness, have been developed by the multinational pharmaceutical industry. These potent products have proven to be of inestimable worth to millions. Not that they are perfect, or work effectively and specifically in every instance. Far from it, unfortunately. But we are getting closer to the dream of a "silver bullet" that will zero in on the specific cellular or even subcellular site to correct the disturbances of brain cell functioning that seem to lie at the root of most mental illnesses. Advancements in research on brain chemistry and physiology and on the function of chemical neurotransmitters in the brain are speeding the day when physicians will have available effective drugs that are specific in correcting the biochemical lesion or lesions concerned, for the patient concerned, without the deleterious side effects which too often limit the effectiveness of therapy today. I have no doubt that such discoveries, which we are already beginning to see, will result in striking advances in the therapy of mental illness over the next decade. I long for that day to come.

Fortunately, there are a number of nonmedication tools that can be used in the treatment of brief or even chronic forms of mental illness. Such therapies most often involve psychotherapy. Examples include cognitive behavioral therapy (CBT), in which a therapist works with a patient to help him or her understand incorrect thought patterns and to reroute the patient's mental energies along more profitable lines. This therapy enhances the patient's potential to endure or possibly recover from a bout of mental illness. Supportive therapy, in which the therapist focuses on providing hope and encouragement for the patient, is yet another useful form of nonmedication therapy.

Tragically, the myths surrounding mental illness impede understanding and foster bias, prejudice, and social stigmatization against those who suffer from this grievous problem. At times, individuals burdened with mental illness may victimize themselves by believing these myths, further intensifying their despair. Dispelling the myths requires their replacement with truth and proper perspective. With knowledge and understanding come love, acceptance, and empathy. These things enhance the ability to endure and foster hope. May God bless us to love *all* His children; to abandon none; to bear each other's burdens; and to lift up, strengthen, and dry the tears of those in pain and suffering.

Many who suffer from mental illness exhibit profound anxiety. Let us turn now to a brief examination of the constellation of illnesses we call anxiety disorders.

Chapter Three

ANXIETY DISORDERS: PARALYZED WITH FEAR

Each of us experiences anxiety, and within limits it's a good thing we do. Anxiety is a widely held emotion in the animal kingdom, as anyone knows who has had the family dog hide under the bed in a thunderstorm. Anxiety and its handmaiden, fear, alert us to potentially dangerous situations and prompt us to avoid or overcome them. If you wake in the middle of the night and hear an unexpected noise downstairs, you're immediately on the alert, without even thinking of it. Your senses go into overdrive, your heart rate speeds up, your hearing and eyesight become more acute. Though you're probably afraid, you (perhaps falteringly) go and investigate what's going on. Your brain activity actually increases, as brain-imaging studies show, and your ability to concentrate and make decisions quickly is enhanced. All your "fight or flight" mechanisms go on alert.

That kind of anxiety helps ensure our survival, just as it did in ancient times when the enemies, or at least the threats, were different in kind if not quantity than they are nowadays. In this chapter I'm not talking about beneficial anxiety, which actually helps us as individuals and society as a whole to live by the rules. Just think how many people would break the law in one way or another if they did not fear the consequences of doing so.

In this chapter I'm referring to anxiety at such levels that it debilitates, paralyzes, or even kills. I'm talking about anxiety for no evident rhyme or reason; anxiety in response to seemingly ordinary events, of such intensity that there is no reasonable explanation for it; anxiety secondary to recurrent uninvited intrusive thoughts and worries; and emotional or physical "flashbacks" that punctuate the recall of previous traumatic events. An example of the consequences of this type of anxiety is found in the student who is beside himself with worry that he will not do well on a test. Subsequently, he becomes paralyzed and unable to think as his body and emotions become flooded with visual and cognitive responses to this perceived imminent danger. His mind and body distracted and disturbed by these fears, he becomes the victim of a self-fulfilling prophecy.

Experts tell us there are several different types of anxiety disorders, some of which severely limit the ability of the sufferer to function effectively or to get any enjoyment out of life. These are not trivial ailments. About one in four Americans will have an anxiety disorder during his or her lifetime. These disorders crush and may destroy their victims. They can make the lives of those they afflict a living nightmare, a suffocating prison. They seem to increase the likelihood the sufferer may turn to alcohol or other mood-modifying drugs in an attempt to deaden the physiologic and psychic pain involved. Perhaps one in six sufferers from severe anxiety may commit suicide. Anxiety disorders definitely are *not* minor illnesses. Experts estimate that up to one-third of anxiety sufferers essentially are disabled and unable to function effectively. A high percentage of people with panic disorder also experience major depression.

Experts list six different anxiety disorders. They include *generalized anxiety disorder; panic disorder* (with or without a fear of crowds, agoraphobia); and *social phobias* (in which patients exhibit anxiety attacks only in the context of social situations, such as a stage fright so profound that it prevents performance and differs from less severe stage fright or "butterflies" that "pump them up" and motivate them to do their best). Social phobias can cause physical symptoms—heart pounding, chest pain, sweating, shaking—so debilitating that victims just can't go on, and they find relief only if they remove themselves from the social situation.

There also are *specific phobias*—fear of snakes, or spiders, or closed-in spaces (claustrophobia), and so on. I once knew someone who was so afraid of snakes that she would faint if she even saw one. Specific phobias can have a very serious impact on a person's life. Someone who has a phobia against black cats, for example, such that he cannot leave his home for fear of meeting one, effectively becomes crippled and imprisoned by his anxiety reaction. No one really knows what causes most specific phobias, although some arise after a discrete traumatic event, such as being bitten by a dog. Some people react to the sight of blood, a phobia so strong they "keel over." I once had a professional colleague who had been a very brave aviator in World War II, having survived three horrendous crashes in combat situations. His physical courage could never be questioned, but if he had to have his finger pricked to take a drop of blood for research purposes, he would faint dead away. Experts now believe such individuals inherit an abnormality in the function of the vagus nerve, one of the body's vital control mechanisms. Stimulation of the vagus nerve can alter heart rate, blood pressure, and even the distribution of blood to various organs within the body. Persons with blood phobias, such as the World War II veteran mentioned, inherit an abnormality which makes their vagus nerve "fire" erratically when they see blood. Their blood pressure drops sharply, and that makes them faint. They don't have a specific phobia, such as fear of spiders or enclosed spaces. Theirs clearly is a physiological problem, not one of psychological origin.

Finally, there are two other serious anxiety disorders, *obsessive-compulsive disorder* (OCD) and *post-traumatic stress disorder* (PTSD), which must also be mentioned.

Persons with obsessive-compulsive disorder experience persistent, intrusive thoughts or impulses which they know are inappropriate but can't control. They have increasing anxiety regarding these events and are ineffective at stopping them despite their best attempts to do so. They may or may not perform repetitive behaviors, often in an attempt to neutralize the anxieties associated with these thoughts or impulses.

Post-traumatic stress disorder comes consequent to a horrific event most commonly not planned or sought after by the individual. The trauma and suffering experienced by the victim of such an event leaves a "scar" of physiologic memory on the individual's brain. Thereafter, elements of the event (e.g., odors, sounds, or association with person[s] who perpetrated the trauma) can trigger a "flashback" of the event, immersing the individual in a cognitive/visceral reliving of the trauma. Sometimes such a flashback can occur without any environmental cue. Needless to say, victims of this disorder live in a state of anxiety that can dramatically alter their lives and adversely affect family members and friends.

GENERALIZED ANXIETY DISORDER

The person with generalized anxiety disorder is more or less always anxious. By definition the anxiety must have persisted for at least six months, but many of those involved have been anxious for as long as they can remember, from early childhood on. The victims worry excessively and unrealistically about almost everything, to such an extent that it interferes with their ability to function normally. They get little joy out of life. The worries are constant and may be focused on every aspect of life: employment, family life, relationships, health, a child's report card, the stock market, tomorrow's weather, and on and on and on. The person broods, worries, fusses, and ruminates incessantly. The afflicted person may suffer from physical ailments, such as headaches, bellyaches, muscle and back problems, and insomnia. These individuals often seek out their family physician in sincere attempts to resolve their complaints. Such attempts to be cured often fail, however, due to the emotional underpinnings of the symptoms. Most persons with generalized anxiety disorder don't get help for what experts believe is the root cause of this common medical illness—brain-cued physiologic responses that generate a variety of distressing and painful physical symptoms.

Benzodiazepine drugs, such as Valium or Librium, give temporary relief of the symptoms in some patients with generalized anxiety, but carry with them the risk of potential addiction. Dependence on these drugs may develop from their use over time. Once a person develops such a dependency, he or she may experience physical and emotional anxiety when attempts are made to stop or even reduce the amount of drug taken. Abrupt withdrawal from benzodiazepine medications may cause a medical emergency, requiring prompt and proper medical care.

Many persons with generalized anxiety disorder have had it for so long they don't even comprehend that anything is wrong with them. Some resort to the use of alcohol or other drugs to quell their anxieties. Others may lapse into serious bouts of depression and end up killing themselves out of a feeling of total helplessness and despair. Interestingly, certain antidepressant drugs recently have been shown to be effective treatments for generalized anxiety disorders.

PANIC DISORDER

Although as many as perhaps 30 percent of the general population will have a single panic attack sometime in their lives, those with genuine panic disorder experience such attacks over and over again, often daily, or even several times a day. The fear that another attack is out there somewhere, about to pounce, may cause afflicted persons to remain in a state of persistent and unremitting fear. They experience a vicious "fear of fear" cycle. In the United States, between two and three percent of adults are affected by panic disorder, and women are three times more likely to develop it than are men. Over time, the sufferer may come to associate the catastrophic series of events involved with an ever-growing list of social situations, which the person feels must be avoided at all cost. Life closes in on the victim, as fewer and fewer situations can be tolerated without fear and panic. Panic disorders then may give rise to agoraphobia, literally fear of the *agora,* the name of the marketplace in ancient Greece. Persons with agoraphobia fear crowded, open areas such as markets, restaurants, streets, subways, or shopping centers. They try to cope with their irrational fear by avoiding such places as often as they can. Although panic attacks and agoraphobia may be concurrent events, some persons with agoraphobia have not, however, had panic attacks previously.

The symptoms of panic disorder include repeated bouts of intense fear and anxiety, which occur suddenly and peak within a few minutes, with episodes usually lasting from ten to thirty minutes. The heart races; the person hyperventilates, trembles, and feels as though he or she is choking or is having a heart attack due to chest pains, nausea, and difficulty breathing. In the midst of an attack, the afflicted person may feel as though he or she is about to die, go crazy, or do something totally out of control, such as drive a car off a cliff. There commonly is a more or less constant anticipatory anxiety about when the next attack will occur. Victims fear they will have an attack in a place or under circumstances where they can't be helped by others, and consequently develop phobic avoidance by striving to keep away from such events and places. Some experts believe that the greater problem in panic disorder is the fear of having an attack, not the attack itself. Others, more biologically and less behaviorally oriented, feel that the panic attack is biologically based and results in the disorder. Experts on both sides of this question agree, however, that the attack starts and drives the illness.

Completely aside from the three classical components to the panic disorder syndrome—the attack itself, anticipatory anxiety, and phobic avoidance—panic disorder often results in serious complications. One is that many physicians often fail to recognize what is happening to the person, and hence she or he doesn't get properly treated. A person afflicted with the disorder may show up repeatedly at a hospital emergency room with what appears at first glance to be a heart attack. Phobic avoidance may effectively shut down the individual's life, by restricting the victim to a "safe" place, typically the home. Work, social life, parenting, and much else just collapse. Victims who turn to alcohol or other drugs for relief find these don't consistently block the attacks and often just introduce other problems, including addiction. Many patients with panic disorder (as many as 50 percent) go on to develop serious depression, with its constant threat of suicide.

Panic disorders certainly run in families. Some experts have postulated a defective gene. Perhaps the most likely explanation for panic disorder (and this is a fiercely debated issue among experts) will be found to be the combination of someone with a biological predisposition who runs up against a highly stressful pattern of life circumstances.

Panic Disorder—A Sufferer's Tale

A few years ago the *Ensign* magazine published a number of short articles by anonymous authors concerning various aspects of mental illness (see "Light in Darkness" 16–21). One of those articles was written by my major consultant in the preparation of this book, our daughter Mary, who described her struggles with panic disorder. That article, recounting a sufferer's trail of tears, is presented below. First, however, may I say that failure to provide the names of authors, although undoubtedly well-meaning, inadvertently perpetuates the stigmatization of mental illness. It implies, however innocently, that mental illness is something shameful, not to be connected with a real person with a real name.

Now, having gotten that off my chest, here is the article:

The first signs of my severe psychological disorder appeared when I was 16. My family had just moved from Canada to England, and I felt like I was stepping into a whole new world.

I attended a private, all-girls school, complete with uniforms, curtseys, and walking practice. At first this seemed charming and unique, but after several weeks the strict routine became almost unbearable; my Canadian schooling had done little to prepare me for the rigors of a traditional British education.

Although I did well in school, I struggled desperately, both intellectually and emotionally. There were hours of homework every night, textbooks of totally unfamiliar material, and few friends.

After months of this stress, I became almost totally unable to function. The thought of attending school or church filled me with indescribable terror.

"Please don't make me go," I pled with my parents. Although they didn't understand what was happening, they reluctantly acquiesced.

"What is happening to you?" they asked.

I didn't know. All I knew was that terror and fear were

taking over my life. These episodes became more and more frequent. My heart would race; I would hyperventilate; tears would stream down my face; I was excessively agitated. Perhaps what I remember most were the feelings of extreme emotional agony. I felt as though my heart, my soul, were being ripped in two.

Soon even leaving the house became an agonizing ordeal. My world became ever smaller and smaller as, consumed by fear, I blocked off more and more facets of normal life.

Fairly soon after arriving in England, I had felt a strong urge to get my patriarchal blessing. I remember the sweet blessing of love and guidance that was poured out upon me. I was promised many wonderful things: marriage to a righteous young man, children to cherish, academic success, the opportunity to use my talents in the service of God.

But there was one paragraph that seemed ominous and foreboding, discussing a profound darkness that would be part of my life. When I received my blessing, I didn't understand that paragraph; now I was beginning to. I struggled to obey the commandments, to read the scriptures, and to pray regularly in order to find guidance, answers, and comfort. I spent many nights crying and begging the Lord for relief and help.

A loving Heavenly Father answered my prayers—not with the healing that I so desperately prayed for but with other blessings. At times when I needed it most I felt the Spirit of the Holy Ghost. Small answers came, enough to get me through each day. My patriarchal blessing became a precious possession.

Included in our family and personal prayers were petitions for guidance in finding medical help. It took time and patience and visits to several doctors before we finally found solid answers. After several years I found a doctor who assured me I wasn't going crazy or losing my mind. What was happening to me, he explained, had a medical description. I was suffering from panic disorder with agoraphobia. I remember my feelings as I heard those words: acute relief mixed with alarm. The diagnosis sounded serious, severe. I was right.

As the psychiatrist detailed the symptoms, I knew immediately that his diagnosis was correct. Finally I could be cured, I thought. After all, wasn't being diagnosed half the battle?

I moved forward with hope, but I would soon learn that for me a "correct diagnosis" wouldn't necessarily result in a cure.

The psychiatrist wrote out a prescription for an anti-anxiety drug, and I began a round of psychotherapy at once. Feeling optimistic, I started school.

Again, however, I began to do well academically, then fell apart emotionally. I spent hours huddled in my parents' closet in tears. Twice I blacked out, and I began trembling and shaking. Finally I was taken to a local psychiatric hospital. My two and a half weeks there probably saved my life. I started a new course of drugs and learned more about feelings, relationships, and communication.

When I left the hospital, I was more stable than I had been for many months. There was a temporary surge of optimism; surely I must be getting well. I entered school again, and once again, within months, my life began to crumble. The panic, the terror crashed in on me. I withdrew from my classes and returned home.

I could now see that my situation was complex and it would take time to find answers. I was despondent. "Dear Heavenly Father," I pled, "please take this illness from me. I have been sick for four years. I look around at the people my age and see them achieving everything that I dream of: school, marriage, a career. I am disabled. I know nothing but intense pain. Why is this happening to me?"

It's been almost five years since my withdrawal from school, and frustratingly little has changed. I suffer severe bouts of clinical depression and have signs of obsessive-compulsive disorder. There are times, all too frequent, when

41

life seems hopeless and my burdens too heavy to bear. I worry about my future: Will I ever marry, be able to return to school, learn to drive, live away from home, feel comfortable at church?

Yet through it all I have felt my Heavenly Father's Spirit, his guidance, his love. Despite periods of despair and darkness, he has blessed me with the courage and light necessary to continue on. In my illness I have been given many things: a loving and supportive family, some understanding friends, my patriarchal blessing, and a wonderful psychiatrist.

Through the past nine years, I have learned tremendous lessons of patience, faith, and empathy. Never again will I take for granted the most supreme gifts of health and peace. My problems haven't been taken from me, but I have been given the resources to cope with them.

I wish I could tell readers Mary has come to the end of her trail of tears. Sadly, this has not occurred as yet. She has gone on, as so many panic disorder patients do, to develop major recurrent depression. She may go for a week or more without symptoms, but the pain keeps coming back, and she fears it may always do so. Instead of hoping for a cure, she hopes now only to endure to the end in faith. Her courage is sublime; her faith in God's will complete. From her suffering has come understanding and wisdom.

OBSESSIVE-COMPULSIVE DISORDER (OCD)

This disorder, which can be one of the most severe psychiatric disorders encountered, was mentioned in passing in chapter 1. Patients with OCD exhibit one or both of two key symptoms: obsessions and compulsions. As indicated previously, obsessions are repetitive, senseless thoughts, which are never realistic, and which play and replay over and over again in the patient's mind. Characteristically, if the patient tries to suppress the urge to obsess on one thing or another, he or she experiences overwhelming anxiety. This goes away only if the victim "gives in" and goes through the obsessive process. Tragically, the obsessions themselves cause anxiety. The victim's disorder markedly interferes with his or her ability to function at work, at home, or socially.

The compulsive component of OCD involves repetitive actions or behaviors, which the victim feels compelled to perform. The classical example involves the patient who repetitively washes and rewashes her hands, several times an hour, because she can't get the idea out of her head that she is dirty or germ-laden. She may literally wash the skin off her hands. The washing characteristically is not just a quick gesture under a running tap, but has to be done ritualistically, in a specified way, in a specified sequence. If there is any break in the routine, that is, if she misses any of the steps involved, the whole process has to be started all over again.

Another person with OCD whom I know had to cook every bit of food she ate for three hours and thirty-three minutes. It didn't matter what the food was—everything from microwaveable popcorn to roast turkey had to be cooked for precisely three hours and thirty-three minutes. No exceptions were allowed. Problems, of course, ensued, including a serious house fire.

Another person could walk down a sidewalk only if she stepped on the concrete slabs in a specific way. All cracks in the concrete had to be avoided with great care, and on every fourth slab she had to lead off with her left foot. She really believed "step on a crack; you'll break your mother's back," and had to prevent that from happening, so she thought, by being scrupulously and meticulously careful where she stepped, to an obsessive degree. The false idea that some repetitive ritual will ward off evil and prevent bad things from happening is also common in OCD sufferers.

It must be made clear that persons with OCD are not psychotic. They have not broken with reality. They know that what they're doing is odd, and not justified by any real need. But if they don't respond to the recurring compulsion to wash and rewash, for example, they become overwhelmed by anxiety.

In his informative book *Brain Lock,* Jeffrey M. Schwartz, M.D., lists several common categories of obsessions and compulsions suffered by those with OCD. They include the following:

Obsessions
- obsessions about dirt and contamination
- obsessive need for order or symmetry
- obsessions about hoarding or saving
- obsessions with sexual content
- repetitive rituals
- - nonsensical doubts
- religious obsessions
- obsessions with aggressive content
- superstitious fears

Compulsions
- cleaning and washing compulsions
- compulsions about having things just right
- hoarding or collecting compulsions

- checking compulsions
- a broad range of other compulsions, including the need for constant reassurance, fixed bedtime rituals to "ward off" evil, excessive list-making, etc.

Dr. Schwartz points out that Howard Hughes, the eccentric millionaire, apparently suffered from severe OCD. By the end of his life, in 1976, Hughes spent his days in isolation in a Mexican hotel, sealed up in a hospital-like atmosphere, terrified of germs. All sunlight had to be blocked from his room because Hughes felt that it transmitted the germs he feared. His food, precisely cut and measured, had to be handled by persons with protective covering on their hands so Hughes would be free from germs. Hughes was the prisoner of an insatiable monster, which in his day could not be treated effectively. Even with all his money he could not defeat the false messages coming from his brain (*Brain Lock,* xi–xii).

The real problem with untreated OCD is that no matter what the person does in response to what he or she is obsessing about, the problem doesn't go away. The urge, and the compulsion to respond in some bizarre way or another, persist, repeatedly intruding into the person's mind. In fact, the word *obsession* comes from a Latin word meaning "to besiege." And that describes what happens to the person with OCD—his mind is besieged. His brain doesn't work properly. It acts as though it were stuck in a gear from which it can't be shifted—hence Dr. Schwartz's felicitous phrase "brain lock." The *form* of OCD—the unrelenting barrage of recurring thoughts and worries—almost certainly has a biological basis and is caused by an improper functioning of the cells in the brain. In contrast, the *content* of OCD—why one person has a compulsion to wash and rewash, and another to repeatedly check to determine if a door really is locked—may well result from emotional factors in an individual's background or family circumstances. But the form of the disease—its underlying cause—clearly is biological in origin. There certainly are emotional aspects as well because OCD results in significant feelings of personal insecurity and stress, which unfortunately extend beyond the sufferer to those around him or her.

OCD affects as many as three percent of Americans. If left untreated, it is likely to last for a lifetime. As mentioned in the introduction to this book (page xi), behavioral modification, either alone or in combination with medication, can be effective in the treatment of OCD. The brain lock *can* be broken.

POST-TRAUMATIC STRESS DISORDER (PTSD)

PTSD always begins with terrible, actual events in a person's life. By definition, those events are not the common misfortunes of living. They must be almost indescribably horrible—seeing your best friend killed in battle, being raped, being the sole survivor in a car crash which kills several people, witnessing the butchering of a Kosovar village. These are examples of the terrible tragedies that trigger the development of PTSD. Perhaps immediately after the event, but perhaps not for several months, the victim develops the two characteristic symptoms of PTSD—flashbacks and emotional numbing. In flashbacks, the victim feels as though he or she is reexperiencing the original horror, over and over again. The emotional numbing involves a general dampening down of emotions, such that the person with PTSD simply doesn't have a full range of feelings.

46

But what about so-called repressed memories, about which the person involved has no memory at all until "primed" by someone, perhaps a therapist? This is a controversial field. Some therapists believe that repressed memories of sexual abuse as a child may produce PTSD in adulthood. I do not pretend to be an expert in this area. As a general principle, however, it would seem wise to be *very* cautious about accepting as real something about which you have absolutely no memory at all. Persons with emotional problems should not let themselves be talked into anything. They must not allow themselves to "remember" something that they don't remember themselves and which in reality may never have happened.

This phenomenon of repressed memory can be very difficult for bishops and other ecclesiastical leaders to deal with. They should seek counsel on this matter from the staff of LDS Family Services or from a trusted, proven, faithful Latter-day Saint professional.

Many persons with mental illness are not anxious, but depressed. I turn now to a brief discussion of that topic.

Chapter Four

THE BLACK DOG
OF DEPRESSION

The title for this chapter comes from Winston Churchill's graphic description of his own feelings of hopelessness, which plagued him all his life. "In times of disappointment, rejection, or bereavement, feelings of hopelessness overwhelmed him. Thoughts of self-destruction were never far away. He told his doctor: 'I don't like standing near the edge of a platform when an express train is passing through. I like to stand back and if possible to get a pillar between me and the train. I don't like to stand by the side of a ship and look down into the water. A second's action would end everything.' He also disliked sleeping near a balcony. He explained: 'I've no desire to quit this world, but thoughts, desperate thoughts, come into the head'" (William Manchester, *The Last Lion*, 19–20).

Churchill learned, to a remarkable degree, to cope with "the black dog" as he termed his spells of brooding depression. He found respite in prodigious activity, the company of flamboyant, exciting people, writing, painting, even bricklaying. Despite his depressive spells—from which he was never really free for very long—he was, by all counts, the greatest Englishman and one of the greatest souls of the twentieth century. Those who are depressed, take heart!

Indeed, depression is common among great people. Among its sufferers have been Johann von Goethe, Abraham Lincoln, Otto von Bismarck, Martin Luther, Oliver Cromwell, Meriwether Lewis, Count Lev Tolstoy, William T. Sherman, and Robert E. Lee. Interestingly, as Manchester notes, Churchill's father and five of the seven dukes of Marlborough, his ancestors, also had depression. Genetic predisposition plays a role in this disease, as in so many others, though the exact nature of that role is still not known. But it is not only the great who are prone to depression. In the United States alone, more than 17 million people experience depression each year, and nearly two-thirds do not get the help they need. In fact, more than one in ten people will suffer a serious depression at some time during their lives.

TYPES OF DEPRESSION

We must clearly differentiate major depression from the transient sadness we all feel during the normal ups and downs of life. Everyone feels sad from time to time. It is natural that we weep at the loss of a loved one; are saddened when something bad happens to us or to someone we love; or grieve when we lose a job, or get sick, or suffer any of the multitude of adversities that inevitably come into every life. It would, in fact, be unhealthy if we did not do so.

Serious depression, however, is something different. It is to ordinary garden-variety sadness as a malignancy is to a hangnail. It takes on a life of its own. It can be all-consuming, seemingly never-ending. It is not amenable to cheering up. The best of news is greeted either with apathy or indifference. It can also be life threatening. A high percentage of people who kill themselves are depressed, and every person who is seriously depressed must be considered at risk for suicide. Serious depression occasionally disappears by itself, but usually some sort of treatment is required. It tends to be a recurrent illness that even if resolved, may occur again, if the constellation of conditions that cause it come together once more in the life of the person involved. About one-third of patients with a single episode of major depression have another within a year after treatment is stopped, and fully half will have a recurrence during their lifetimes.

Like many other illnesses—cancer, heart disease, or pneumonia, for example—depression is not a single disorder. It exhibits numerous forms, with different characteristics, which require different treatments. Jack M. Gorman, M.D., in his authoritative book *The Essential Guide to Mental Health*, lists five main types of depression (177–84). The first is called *major depression,* a condition characterized by a "nonreactive" mood in the patient, who simply cannot be cheered up by anything. Persons with major depression have disturbed sleep patterns, often awakening very early, and being unable to get back to sleep. They lose their appetite, have no interest in food, and consequently lose weight. They look sad and pained. They walk and talk slowly and hesitantly. They are unable to concentrate or think clearly, are fatigued and have little energy, and believe life is not worth living. They frequently fantasize about death and dying. Some commit suicide. They often blame

51

themselves for some trivial thing or another and spend hours in guilty, obsessive ruminations. They may feel they should be punished for something or other, which they haven't done, or for some deed so inconsequential as not to be worthy of mention. Major depression is a serious, potentially life-threatening illness. Treatment usually is required before improvement is seen.

Bipolar depression is part of a mood disorder called bipolar disorder, in which the patient has alternating periods of deep depression and manic euphoria, usually separated by periods of normal moods. Bipolar disorder commonly starts earlier in life than major depression, often in the early twenties. There is general consensus that bipolar disorder is a genetic illness that runs in families and almost certainly is of biological origin. The depressions into which bipolar patients sink often are extremely deep, and as many as 25 percent of patients will kill themselves, or at least attempt to do so unless treated.

The ravages wrought by bipolar disorder are illustrated by the following two examples of Rob Stock and Sharlene Kuehnl:

Rob's Story

In Kentucky [Rob Stock], was senior class president and a soccer star. He landed a scholarship to a university in Colorado.

Rob gave up his scholarship, blew all his money, and returned home.

His mother, Teri, wondered if her son was experimenting with drugs. She took him to see a doctor, who told her, "You'd better pray it is drugs, because if it's mental illness, you're in for a ride."

When the diagnosis was made, Teri had no choice but to climb on.

Bipolar disorder, formerly known as manic-depressive illness, usually strikes between the ages of 19 and 24.

"We've been in the system for five years. There's been seven suicide attempts, one right after he got out of the hospital. The good news is he took his medication. The bad news? He took 50."

The pictures of her family on her baby grand piano don't tell that story.

There's one of Rob and the pretty blonde girl he took to the prom. He looks confident and handsome.

"One day, he had the world at his feet, and then it was all taken away. The day I found out he was bipolar I refer to as the day my son died. The son I loved—at times I see glimpses of him."

Rob checked himself in to the hospital in March when he felt a downward spiral begin. His mother is grateful he recognized it. But the flip side of that dawning consciousness comes with its own kind of misery.

"When he can articulate his pain, he asks me to give him something to live for. What do I tell him?"

Rob's little sister made him a scrapbook, compiling newspaper articles about his soccer career, photos from grade schools, notices of academic achievement, and his certificate of Aaronic Priesthood ordination.

He cried. It took him two years to look at it.

His mother understands.

"Since he was 19, the only thing I have to put in there is hospital reports."

Sharlene's Story

Sharlene Kuehnl's bipolar daughter was arrested for assaulting her boyfriend.

"She can be very violent and mean, but as long as she is on her medication she is wonderful," her mother said.

Keuhnl called the jail where her daughter was incarcerated.

She said her daughter was mentally ill and that she hoped she would receive the right kind of medications.

She didn't.

"When I hear her on the phone panicking and crying, it makes you feel so hopeless," Kuehnl said. "You feel helpless anyway. It is hard enough when they are young and they have a cold. Then mental illness comes along and a cold would be wonderful compared to this." (Bryson, "Mental Illness Hijacks Families," C 2).

Psychotic depression is a variant of major depression, but the sufferer develops hallucinations, delusions, or both. These breaks with reality often involve auditory hallucinations, in which the patient hears voices when no one is talking. These voices actually seem to the sufferer as if someone is speaking, often telling the victim that he or she is a terrible person who deserves to die or be punished.

The delusions experienced in psychotic depression have no basis in reality. They are depressive in their nature—the person has fixed and false beliefs, which he or she can't be talked out of. The themes of these delusions often spring from the depressed person's entrenched repetitive thought processes (a way of thinking known as rumination). They often involve endless thoughts of guilt, unrelenting hopelessness, and a conviction others do not like the depressed individual. The delusional thought process whips up these preoccupations to a fever pitch, and the person loses his or her ability to distinguish what is real and what is not. To the person with psychotic depression, his or her distorted, delusional thoughts are the only reality. These delusions, which psychiatrists call "mood congruent," do not necessarily indicate to the sufferer that he or she is famous or brilliant, however. On the contrary, they often indicate to the psychotically depressed person that he or she is infamous and totally depraved.

In *atypical depression,* the sufferer usually can be cheered up, in contrast to the patient with a major depression, who can't. Those with atypical depression maintain some reactivity of mood, meaning their moods can be brightened by exposure to external events previously found to be enjoyable. That mood improvement, however, is only temporary. Once the pleasurable external event has ended, the patient slides back down into the blackness of depression, often within hours. Sufferers from atypical depression tend to overeat and oversleep when depressed and often suffer from interpersonal rejection sensitivity. In other words, they are very sensitive to rejection and criticism. This form of depression, like others, can develop into a chronic challenge for its sufferers.

Dysthymia is the technical term used to describe persons who are more or less depressed for most of the day, for more days than not, for at least two years. These people retain the ability to function, even though they often feel "down in the dumps." They may be so used to being depressed that they think, *That's just the way I am; there's nothing wrong with me.*

The type of depression from which one suffers determines the type of treatment that mental health professionals will prescribe.

THE ORIGINS OF DEPRESSION

It is beyond the scope of this book to discuss in any detail the cause of depression. Suffice it to say there are three popular theories as to its origin: psychoanalytic, cognitive/behavioral, and biological (genetic theories fall into this third category). All theoretically are powerful and compelling, but none of them alone can account for all aspects of the illness of depression. Indeed, many who treat depression use a three-pronged approach, taking into careful account the psychological, social, and biological components involved in this illness. For example, even though there is good evidence that depression runs in families, it is not certain how much is inherited (or at least predisposes a person to depression) and how much is learned from being around depressed family members for many years. We simply are not yet able to separate nature from nurture in depression.

Additionally, although there is intriguing evidence that depression has something, probably a great deal, to do with neurotransmitters (norepinephrine, serotonin, and perhaps numerous others) in the brain, our understanding of the ways in which brain cells communicate with each other is still in its infancy. A major problem lies in the fact it is extremely difficult to measure neurotransmitter levels at the point of the individual neuron (nerve cell) in the brain. It does seem certain that one *cannot* fully explain depression by hypothesizing that it is caused *simply* by low brain levels of neurotransmitters and can therefore effectively be treated by increasing neurotransmitter levels by use of drugs. Whatever is happening at a cellular level during antidepressant therapy appears to be more complicated.

Indeed, some researchers believe that the influence of antidepressants on the concentration of neurotransmitters outside of the nerve cell (the neuron) promotes actual changes in the cell itself. According to this theory, in effect the nerve cell is restructured into a more functional state in patients given anti-depressants. As much as this idea helps explain why many antidepressants take several weeks to exert their effect, it remains a theory, however, and the exact mechanisms by which antidepressants influence depression are still incompletely understood.

DEPRESSION IN CHILDREN AND TEENS

There are many who believe that depression is strictly an adult disease, but we know this is not so. Even preadolescent children can be seriously depressed and in need of help. Statistics indicate that nearly 2 percent of children ages 7–12 in the United States have major depression ("Depression in Children," 2).

A case in point is described in an article by Jan Underwood Pinborough: "A ten-year-old boy . . . became profoundly depressed in the years following his mother's death. When his father began to date again, the child withdrew, lost weight, and began having trouble in school. [A faithful Latter-day Saint physician] found there was a strong history of depression on the mother's side of the family. He taught the family how to help the child feel secure in his new family situation. He also prescribed an antidepressant medication for the child. The child eventually recovered" ("Mental Illness," 55).

The tragic tale of depressed children is played out daily in every part of the globe. Children, the innocent victims of violence, civil war, or intense ethnic hatred, become depressed in response to the extreme stresses they are faced with daily—the loss of parents and siblings, blood and horror on all sides, physical or sexual abuse or both, disruption of life, family separation, perhaps even mutilation or other injuries to themselves. In every land, the death or divorce of parents, failure to establish emotional bonds in infancy because of neglect and rejection, excessive punishment, or the presence of depressed parents in the home all probably contribute to the development of depression in children. President Gordon B. Hinckley's somber words of rebuke regarding child abuse and neglect bear repetition: "Such abuse is not new. There is evidence to indicate that it goes back through the ages. It is a most despicable and tragic and terrible thing. I regret to say that there has been some very limited expression of this monstrous evil among us [i.e., among Latter-day Saints]. It is something that cannot be countenanced or tolerated. The Lord Himself said, 'But whoso shall offend one of these little ones which believe in me, it were better for him that a millstone were hanged about his neck, and that he were drowned in the depth of the sea' (Matthew 18:6).

"That is very strong language from the Prince of Peace, the Son of God."

President Hinckley continues: "I quote from our *Church Handbook of Instructions:* 'The Church's position is that abuse cannot be tolerated in any form. Those who abuse . . . are subject to Church discipline. They should not be given Church callings and may not have a temple recommend. Even if a person who abused a child sexually or physically receives Church discipline and is later restored to full fellowship or readmitted by baptism, leaders should not call the person to any position working with children or youth unless the First

Presidency authorizes removal of the annotation on the person's membership record.

"'In instances of abuse, the first responsibility of the Church is to help those who have been abused and to protect those who may be vulnerable to future abuse'" (*Book 1: Stake Presidencies and Bishoprics* [1998], 157–58).

President Hinckley continues: "For a long period now we have worked on this problem. We have urged bishops, stake presidents, and others to reach out to victims, to comfort them, to strengthen them, to let them know that what happened was wrong, that the experience was not their fault, and that it need never happen again" ("Personal Worthiness," 52–59).

And President Boyd K. Packer has added his wise counsel on this matter: "Children should not be ignored or neglected. They absolutely must not be abused or molested. Children must not be abandoned or estranged by divorce. Parents are responsible to provide for their children. . . .

"We are to look after their physical, their spiritual, and their emotional needs" ("Children," 8).

The National Institute of Mental Health (NIMH) estimates that as many as 8 percent of teenagers in America suffer from major depression. Each year from 8 to 11 of every 100,000 teens in the United States commit suicide—as many as those who die from all other causes combined. In fact, according to a 1999 survey, approximately one in five high school students in America has seriously considered suicide (Hales and Hales, "When a Teenager Is Sad," 4).

Many teenagers try as best they can to hide their problems from others, even themselves. A recent article by Dianne Hales and Dr. Robert E. Hales describes a young man who put on his "happy face" every morning. He was involved in school activities, the president of his junior class, and a varsity basketball player. But his heart was breaking inside. Whenever he was alone, he cried. He cried himself to sleep at night and woke up crying in the morning. All he wanted to do was to die. Finally, one night, after having helped win a basketball game, he tried to kill himself by overdosing on drugs. Happily, his life was saved.

The teenage years can be and often are years of turbulence as adolescents strive to develop their own independence and identity and make their way in what often is a hostile world. Another teenager described by Hales and Hales was constantly teased by fellow students during her growing-up years in a large American city. She was always able to turn to her beloved grandmother for support and reassurance. But then the grandmother died and the girl felt terribly bereft. More trauma followed: she was sexually assaulted by a boy, and two uncles died within a few weeks of each other.

Her grades plummeted. She lost weight and saw no point in living. When a teacher at her school committed suicide, the teenager finally snapped and went to school officials for help. Fortunately, with medication prescribed for her and counseling for her and her family, improvement soon occurred. Now, a few years later, the young lady looks back on those years of trauma and turbulence as times of learning. She learned in therapy how to express her feelings and to set goals. Her grades at school improved, and she learned to get along better with her mother. But it was a close call. Had she not received help, she might well have either ended her life or gotten into serious difficulties from which she could not have extricated herself.

These two cases illustrate the symptoms often seen in depressed teenagers. These unfortunate youth may not look or act sad on the surface, but each displays telltale signs they are in serious trouble. These warning signs include the following:

- A decline in school grades, problems in concentrating, and difficulties in getting along with teachers or other students.
- Mood changes—irritability, sadness, becoming easily upset or angered; frequent crying "jags"; frequent quarrels with family members and friends; a feeling of empty hopelessness; a desire to die.
- Loss of interest in hobbies, athletics, or social activities; lack of enjoyment in activities that previously were enjoyed.
- Changes in sleep patterns, including insomnia, waking up early and being unable to get back to sleep, or wanting to sleep for excessively long periods.
- Gaining or losing large amounts of weight; fatigue, restlessness, or agitation.
- Excessive feelings of guilt and self-criticism; taking blame for inconsequential things or things that are not really his or her fault.

The possibility that a teenager may take his own life frightens parents, of course. Often, parents are afraid to meet the problem head-on, but failure to do so only increases the chances of irremediable tragedy. The best thing parents can do is to talk openly about the problem to the person involved. Ask him if he has thought of suicide. Be sympathetic, calm, and low-key, assuring the teenager that you understand his pain and suffering and asking him to promise to talk to a parent or some other person before attempting suicide. Most teenagers will keep that promise. They don't really want to die, though they may attempt to do so if they don't get help. Down deep, they want to live, and they have so much to live for.

What then should parents do when they have a depressed teenager? The following will be helpful:

- Most importantly, talk to your child. Let him or her know of your love and how much you want to help. Pray together daily. Don't foolishly assume he or she will grow out of it and that it's only a temporary phase.

- Obtain a priesthood blessing for the teenager with all of the spiritual power it brings. A blessing from a worthy father, grandfather, sibling, or other family member can be of special value by reinforcing the fact this is a family problem and that all family members care deeply about what happens. Repeat the blessing as often as necessary. A blessing from the bishop or other assigned priesthood bearer is, of course, always appropriate.

- Get competent professional help. If possible, seek the services of a competent Latter-day Saint therapist, or if such is not available, a professionally competent person who respects gospel principles. Given the choice of a less-qualified Latter-day Saint or a more qualified non-Latter-day Saint who respects gospel principles, I would choose the latter. This is an area where professional competence counts for a lot. Don't delay getting help: there is some evidence that an untreated depressive episode (whether in an adolescent or an adult) enhances the likelihood of a later recurrence of the illness.

- Lock up medications and remove *all* guns from the home.
- Don't leave the teenager alone for long periods of time.
- Be aware that alcohol, illegal drugs, and cigarettes only exacerbate the problem, and talk to your teenager about his or her vulnerability. These substances often are taken to suppress the symptoms and help the victim blot out symptoms of depression, but they do nothing to help in that or any other respect, and their use only introduces new problems.

Fortunately, most teenagers respond well to antidepressant medication and to cognitive/behavioral therapy, which teaches them how better to deal with stress and unrealistic thinking.

DEPRESSION IN WOMEN

Available evidence indicates that women are about twice as likely as men to experience depression. How much of this difference is biological, stress-related, or due to differences in reporting between the sexes cannot be said with certainty. In any case, the differences are independent of racial and ethnic background or economic status. The higher incidence of depression in females begins to show up in adolescence. Adolescent boys are more likely to develop behavior problems and abuse alcohol or drugs; girls are more likely to become depressed. Women molested as children or raped as adults are more likely to become depressed at some time in their lives, as are those who are physically abused. How wise and sobering are President Gordon B. Hinckley's words: "How tragic and utterly disgusting a phenomenon is wife abuse. Any man in this Church who abuses his wife, who demeans her, who insults her, who exercises unrighteous dominion over her is unworthy to hold the priesthood. Though he may have been ordained, the heavens will withdraw, the Spirit of the Lord will be grieved, and it will be amen to the authority of the priesthood of that man. . . .

"I regret to say that I see too much of this ugly phenomenon. There are men who cuff their wives about, both verbally and physically. What a tragedy when a man demeans the mother of his children. . . .

"My brethren, if there be any within the sound of my voice who are guilty of such behavior, I call upon you to repent. Get on your knees and ask the Lord to forgive you" ("Personal Worthiness," 54).

As with younger age groups, more women than men among the elderly suffer from depression, although suicide rates are highest in elderly white men living alone. Sadly, but perhaps not unexpectedly, two-thirds of widows or widowers have major depression in the first month after the death of their spouse, and half of those remain clinically depressed a year later.

Postpartum Depression

As many as 85 percent of women experience "baby blues" after the birth of a child. These usually occur in the first week after delivery and are characterized by insomnia, sadness, low energy levels, and spontaneous weeping. Usually women experiencing the blues don't need treatment, but they do require a lot of love and support from family and spouse.

Some women, however—10 to 15 percent of those giving birth—go on to develop a major depression in the postpartum period, the onset occurring within four weeks of delivery. They show the signs of depression already noted, and in addition also often have severe anxiety, which may include panic attacks about the new baby. They may have little evident interest in the baby and undergo bouts of spontaneous crying long after the postpartum blues should have been over and done with.

Impoverished, single women who give birth are twice as likely as middle-class, married women to develop postpartum depression. Treatment is similar to that for a major depression, usually including antidepressants and psychotherapy. If the woman is planning to breast-feed her new baby, it is recommended she first consult with her physician. The physician can discuss the risks of exposing the baby to antidepressant medication (via the mother's breast milk) versus the risks of the mother's untreated depression worsening, placing both mother and child in danger.

The most severe mental illness following birth, one which fortunately is rare, involves development of postpartum psychosis, affecting up to two women per 1,000 births. The afflicted woman may have auditory or visual hallucinations (hearing or seeing things that are not there), or delusions, which usually focus on the new baby. An example would be the tragedy, much reported in the media recently, of the Texas mother who drowned her five children to "save" them from the evils of the world. The symptoms of this ailment usually appear within two to three weeks of delivery. This is a serious disorder, and prompt medical attention is required.

Depression among Latter-day Saint women

What about depression among Latter-day Saint women? Certainly membership in the Church does not exempt women from depression. Based on many years of training and experience, Dr. Brent Scharman of LDS Family Services is of the opinion that problems facing Latter-day Saint women in the United States today may actually be more complex and potentially debilitating than those encountered in the past. He points out that life is more complicated and hectic nowadays, with competition in school and on the job; working long hours, often in addition to the primary role as wife and mother; excessive materialism; sensational media reports; increased levels of divorce and family breakup; the challenges of single parenting; and an increase in the availability of drugs, alcohol, and pornography all making a woman's lot in this and other developed countries difficult indeed.

In Dr. Scharman's view, many LDS women, like their sisters who are not Latter-day Saints, struggle with perfectionism, which defines their self-worth too narrowly. Problems of self-esteem; trouble in family relationships; the "learned helplessness" of believing that try as you will, you can't get what you want; and conflict between staying at home with children and working outside the home are all real factors in the lives of women today. If to those stressors one adds biological predisposition to depression, serious problems can result (see S. Brent Scharman, talk at BYU Women's Conference, 3 May 2001).

But Latter-day Saint women have the unparalleled assurances of the Savior to lean upon: "Come unto me, all ye that labour and are heavy laden, and I will give you rest. Take my yoke upon you, and learn of me; for I am meek and lowly in heart: and ye shall find rest unto your souls. For my yoke is easy, and my burden is light" (Matthew 11:28–30). As Alma said to his son Shiblon: "And now my son, Shiblon, I would that ye should remember, that as much as ye shall put your trust in God even so much ye shall be delivered out of your trials, and your troubles, and your afflictions, and ye shall be lifted up at the last day" (Alma 38:5). Additionally, though life can be difficult, Latter-day Saint women, while by no means immune from the vicissitudes of living, have the wondrous support system of the Church organizations to protect and cushion them. The great, unparalleled sisterhood of Relief Society is a case in point.

Simply put, there is no evidence that Latter-day Saint women are more depressed than those who are not members of the Church. However, a few words of advice to Latter-day Saint women concerning depression may be appropriate.

- Learn to identify your feelings—why you feel as you do and what is causing your feelings. The quicker you do so, the more able you will be to do something about them. Remember that an ounce of prevention is worth a pound of cure.
- Don't beat yourself up over mistakes. Making a mistake doesn't mean you are generally incompetent or a useless good-for-nothing.
- Be around happy people as much as you can, and do all you can to raise your own mood and keep it high.
- Resist the impulse to compare yourself against other women. First, you really can't do so with any degree of accuracy. Second, you don't have to compete with anyone.
- Believe you can learn and change. You may have to reorder your thought patterns, in order to gain better control over your thoughts and behavior, but you can do so.
- Learn to accept the rhythms of life and its natural ups and downs. President Boyd K. Packer's wise counsel bears reading:

"It was meant to be that life would be a challenge. To suffer some anxiety, some depression, some disappointment, even some failure is normal. Teach our members that if they have a good, miserable day once in a while, or several in a row, to stand steady and face them. Things will straighten out. There is great purpose in our struggle in life" ("Solving Emotional Problems," 93).

- Recognize that overcoming depression or other emotional problems usually takes both personal effort and personal revelation, in addition to full utilization of all the resources at one's disposal.

- Since marital discord often precedes the onset of depression, work hard to ensure the strength of your marriage.

- If you feel yourself slipping into depression, get help, both spiritual *and* medical, as soon as possible. Don't delay: it doesn't pay!

- Learn that some things cannot be cured but simply must be endured. As Elder Neal A. Maxwell has said, speaking as one who has himself suffered long and hard, "Some undergo searing developments that cut suddenly into mortality's status quo. Some have trials to *pass through,* while still others have allotments they are to *live with.* Paul lived with his 'thorn in the flesh' (2 Cor. 12:7). Suffice it to say, such mortal allotments will be changed in the world to come. The exception is unrepented sin that shapes our status in the next world" ("Content with the Things Allotted unto Us," 72–74).

- Stay faithful. Pray daily. Read the scriptures and ponder over their meaning in your life. Attend your Church meetings regularly. And always remember, though like Nephi you "do not know the meaning of all things," you may always have the full assurance that God "loveth his children" (1 Nephi 11:17). You will never be alone. His love is constant and eternal. As the Apostle Paul said so long ago: "For I am persuaded, that neither death, nor life, nor angels, nor principalities, nor powers, nor things present, nor things to come, nor height, nor depth, nor any other creature, shall be able to separate us from the love of God, which is in Christ Jesus our Lord" (Romans 8:38–39).

DEPRESSION: A SUFFERER'S TALE

The saga of our daughter Mary's continued suffering goes on:

The story of my long involvement with panic disorder was summarized in chapter 3. As I look back I recognize there were aspects of depression from the beginning of my problems. As occurs with so many victims of panic disorder, my depression has deepened and darkened for the past several years. For me at least, the depression I now suffer is much worse than the anxiety and fear of panic attacks that had already torn my life apart. I seem to be in the middle of a never-ending nightmare of blackness and despair, so fatigued both physically and emotionally I know not where to turn. Many days I long for death. It seems the only doorway open to me. I struggle to endure, battered by depression, anxiety, and obsessive thoughts, which attack me more or less continuously.

As my prayers for relief from the darkness that overwhelms me have not yet been answered, my feelings of guilt and despair have heightened. In my confusion, I think in error that if God doesn't answer me, it must be my fault. I feel, wrongly, that I am a bad and unworthy person, being punished for something I've done. But I've no idea what my sins are, and in more objective moments realize that my feelings of guilt and despair are *symptoms* of my disease, not the causes.

I realize now there is an obsessive component to my illness. It started at school in England, where even during our six-week summer vacation we had homework every day. I vacillated between being angry and resentful because there was never a day of relief from homework and my obsessive anxiety about work that I had not yet completed. And, I thought, in my obsessive perfectionism, I *have* to be at the top of the class.

I realize, though it gives me no comfort, that mine is a case where a biological predisposition to illness combined with very stressful life situations to result in what has been well-nigh unbearable suffering.

I was hospitalized in early 2001 with severe depression. With high hopes I began a series of treatments with electro-convulsive therapy (ECT). This is no longer the frightening ordeal described in *One Flew Over the Cuckoo's Nest,* the sensational movie of 1975, which portrayed ECT as a savage and barbaric treatment for a wide range of mental illnesses, including depression. Attended by a psychiatrist and an anesthesiologist, I was briefly anesthetized and given an electric shock through my head for a few seconds. Since I was anesthetized, I felt nothing. I'm told my foot twitched slightly. After a few minutes, I woke up and was allowed to go home. During a three-week period I underwent eight ECT sessions.

Initially, the ECT seemed to work. I was elated; perhaps, finally, we had stumbled on a cure. But it was not to be: once again my carefully guarded hopes were dashed, destroyed, broken into a million fragments. My depression recurred, as bad as ever. My cynicism about ever finding anything that would help only increased.

The ECT caused permanent memory loss; all of my memories for about a five-month period just before the treatments began are gone, I suppose forever, and my recollections of the previous three years are sketchy at best. I felt dull and stupid—the mental equivalent of walking in sand up to my waist—for about six months. I noticed that my very-short-term memory was disturbed, so that I couldn't remember what I'd said two sentences previously. I'm certain I lost some IQ points. Luckily, my mental acuity has largely come back, but I expect that my memory loss will remain till the end of my days.

I would gladly have traded all my losses, troublesome though they are, for permanent improvement. In skilled hands, ECT does provide relief to many with severe depression. I was one of the unlucky ones—about 20 percent—who just don't respond.

My depression tends to be worse during the gray days of winter, but even in summer there is little tranquillity. Thankfully, I continue to receive high quality care from a skilled and compassionate LDS psychiatrist. He has tried so many different medications that our home medicine cabinet looks like a well-equipped pharmacy. So far we still haven't found anything that works permanently. Some drugs work for a while—even up to a year—and then stop being effective. Others have side effects that for me at least are either so dangerous or noticeable that I have had to discontinue their use. One particularly difficult and potentially dangerous side effect is what is known as *tardive dyskinesia,* in which my tongue trembles and my muscles stiffen and twitch. About a year ago I had a medication-induced grand mal seizure on a long flight of concrete stairs, which nearly killed me. Insomnia has been a recurrent problem, and the tendency of some drugs to produce weight gain—not acceptable for many young women like myself—has required me to stop taking them.

Last summer, in yet another attempt to obtain relief, I visited a nationally renowned psychopharmacologist in California. I had cautious optimism he could help. After all, he supposedly was *the* authority in the field. His interview with me and my parents was abrasive, confrontational, and demeaning. I ended up in tears. Much worse, his prescription for relief, given with such confidence, proved to be of no value at all.

The results of this litany of horrors have been devastating. All aspects of my life have been seriously impacted. Because of unhappy Church experiences in England, where one of my Young Women leaders, without even talking to me, opined that I was unworthy even though in reality I was too frightened to go to church, I've developed phobic avoidance toward church. For several years, the best I could do was to walk in one door of the meetinghouse and out the other. Staying for even five minutes just wasn't possible, even though I longed with all my heart to do so and prayed over and over again for the necessary strength. Some months—but not always—I have been able to stay for the sacrament, fighting back my terrible, overwhelming fear every second of the time.

As my self-confidence has eroded under the unremitting pressures of fear, depression, and guilt, my ability to establish friendships has disappeared. Dating has been difficult at best.

People—not knowing or understanding the extent of my disabilities, but anxious to be friendly—would ask me out to a movie, a party, or some other social event. Time and time again I would agree, but as the hour drew near, I would be choked by fear and doubt and have to back away. Now I have little social self-confidence left. My loneliness is almost more than I can bear.

During one of my hospitalizations, the psychiatric social worker asked, "Who has died in your family; why are you in mourning?" At first I couldn't understand. Nobody had died in our family. But now I know there *has* been a death. In a very real way, *I* am the deceased. My talents, potential dignity, sense of self-worth, hopes for marriage and children—all have been killed by the illness, which has smashed my life. The pain at my multiple losses is something so monstrous I dare not fully plumb its depths. The cruelest cut of all is that I have been passed over in my deepest desires to be a wife and mother.

Mine has been a lonely spiritual labor as well. At times I admit to having been angry at God. *Why* doesn't He lift my burdens? Why do all my pleadings and prayers go unanswered? I plead for His forgiveness and wet my pillow with my tears.

I'm beginning to come to terms with my grief and sense of overwhelming loss and bereavement. Though God has not yet taken away my problems, He *has* given me the means to survive them and reach some sort of peace. I'm beginning to accept that I can't do all I must on my own strength. Christ is the key to my survival and salvation. Though the longed-for miracle may not come in this life, He will walk with me. The words of Luke 6:48 echo often in my mind: "He [or in my case, she] is like [one] which built an house, and digged deep, and laid the foundation on a rock: and when the flood arose, the stream beat vehemently upon that house, and could not shake it: for it was founded upon a rock."

I have full confidence that come what may, I *will* overcome. My foundation is unshakable. Christ is my Rock. Though the floods "beat vehemently" upon me, I *will* withstand whatever happens, no matter how painful it is.

Mary's story is sad and deeply troubling. Fortunately, it is the exception rather than the rule. In the hands of wise and competent mental health professionals, most sufferers from depression can be helped in significant ways to regain their lives. In most instances, medication and/or behavioral therapy can help to lift the blanket of darkness that smothers the depressed person. Electroconvulsive therapy (ECT), while it did not help Mary, is of real value in the treatment of perhaps 80 percent of persons with major depression. So we do not give up hope for a better future for our beloved daughter. We long for it to come.*

One of the most frightening and debilitating mental illnesses, schizophrenia, will be discussed next.

---

* Since the above was written a few months ago, Mary has begun psychotherapy under the direction of a highly skilled and faithful Latter-day Saint clinical psychologist. She is making excellent progress; our hopes are high.

Chapter Five

SCHIZOPHRENIA: DEMONS OF DARKNESS

Schizophrenia is a severe, frequently devastating disease, whose victims commonly are characterized by others as "crazies," "loonies," and "nut-cases" and given other derogatory, untrue, and bigoted labels. The recent award-winning movie *A Beautiful Mind,* which portrayed some aspects of the life of John Nash, a talented university professor who developed schizophrenia (and who later won the Nobel Prize in economics), has helped portray schizophrenics in a more sympathetic light, but prejudice, ignorance, and hostility still characterize the attitudes of many toward schizophrenic patients.

Some of the public fear about schizophrenic persons undoubtedly rises from the fact that schizophrenia causes bizarre symptoms in its victims. Persons with schizophrenia are psychotic; that is, they "break with reality." Hallucinations—usually auditory (hearing voices when no one is speaking)—are common. Visual hallucinations, in which the victim sees things not there, are less common but not unknown. A few patients have tactile hallucinations, usually involving something imaginary crawling over or under their skin. Usually the voices heard are frightening, condemnatory, and critical of the victim. The victim may answer the voice, or voices, since there may be several. The victim appears to be talking to himself, but to him the voices are completely real.

A second psychotic symptom commonly found in schizophrenics is delusions—false, fixed ideas, with no substance in reality. Paranoid delusions involve the victim's believing that someone, or perhaps a vast conspiracy of enemies, or a government agency, or little green men from Mars, is out to get him. They want to kill him, or abduct him, or do weird things to his mind, or are planning to harm him in other ways. The victim may believe the CIA has bugged his television set, has a camera in the light bulb in his kitchen, or is watching him every minute of the day and night from across the street. He may believe that strange alien beings are growing within his body, and he or she can't be persuaded otherwise. The list of delusions is practically endless.

The last of the triumvirate of psychotic symptoms involves disorders of thought so severe the person can't communicate properly. He may not make any sense when he speaks. Much of what he says is gibberish. He may do bizarre things, like wearing layers of heavy winter clothes on a hot summer's day, or standing on a street corner, continuously rotating his head for hours on end. Some of the homeless persons one sees on the streets of any big city likely are suffering from schizophrenia.

In addition to the "positive symptoms" of hallucinations, delusions, and thought disorders, schizophrenic persons also demonstrate so-called "negative symptoms," which represent the decreased ability or drive to initiate normal interpersonal behaviors. Negative symptoms include social withdrawal, lack of facial expression, apathy, inability to get pleasure from anything, and motionless staring into space, perhaps for hours on end. Not uncommonly—Professor Nash to the contrary—over time schizophrenics demonstrate loss of ability to think and to reason. The stereotype of the schizophrenic as the "mad genius" simply isn't true. It is rare indeed for schizophrenics to maintain their predisease intellectual acuity in the face of the devastating departure from reality and the inaccurate interpretations that schizophrenia induces in the minds of those it afflicts.

Experts now agree that schizophrenia is a biological illness. Older theories relating schizophrenia to poor mothering, aberrant social circumstances, or poverty just don't hold up to careful examination. Some cases of schizophrenia, it is now believed, have a genetic origin and result from the inheritance of defective genes, which result in abnormal functioning of the brain. Persons with schizophrenia are much more likely to have close blood relatives with the affliction than are persons without schizophrenia. But there is growing evidence that other cases of schizophrenia are probably caused by some sort of environmental insult that disturbs the development of the brain of the unborn infant. Two parts of the brain—the temporal lobe and the prefrontal cortex—seem to be involved; and two neurotransmitters (brain chemicals involved in communication between brain cells) also are believed to play a role. These two chemicals are called dopamine and serotonin. Research conducted at the National Institute of Mental Health in Washington, D.C., has shown that in identical twins, one with schizophrenia and one not afflicted with the disease, the twin with schizophrenia had a slightly smaller brain than his or her normal sibling. (Cited by Gorman, *The Essential Guide to Mental Health,* 289). The abnormality was most apparent in the temporal lobe of the brain, the area considered responsible for control of emotions and memory. Sophisticated brain-imaging techniques recently have shown that the prefrontal cortex of the brain also develops abnormally, probably during the fourth to sixth months of the mother's pregnancy, in persons who become schizophrenic.

Effective treatment of schizophrenia involves the use of medication; some patients also benefit from psychotherapy. Repeated hospitalizations are common, particularly in patients who do not take their medication regularly. In fact, approximately 25 percent of psychiatric beds in American hospitals are occupied by schizophrenic patients. About one in ten individuals with schizophrenia commits suicide, presumably unable to live any more with the demons, devils, and delusions that haunt him or her.

A recent article in the Salt Lake City *Deseret News* illustrates the horrors undergone by schizophrenic patients and their families. It tells the story of a man named Terrell Sorensen:

> Not long ago, Terrell Sorensen slipped outside and shimmied under his truck while the rest of his family slept. He knew he would find help there. His mind churning and his body in pain from construction accidents, he lay there drinking motor oil. It would lubricate his back, loosen the tumor, and make it slide away.

Later, he disappeared into the mountains and tried to copy the elk and deer. He knew many of them were shot but managed to heal.

If he ate what they did, lived like they did, he would recover.

But he has schizophrenia, not a bullet wound. . . .

Peggy Sorensen knows when her son, Terrell, is on the edge of disaster.

He stops worrying about combs and hair brushes and clothes.

"When he starts worrying about his hair and agrees to get it cut, I know he's getting better."

Terrell's illness began slowly.

Four years ago he had friends, a job, a fiancée. Then little things started to happen.

He broke up with his girlfriend. He started sleeping a lot, retreating to his bedroom for hours, days.

His mother thought it was depression and he'd shake free. He didn't.

She sought help, but Terrell was twenty-six. A mother can only do so much for an adult child, especially when she bumps into the system.

"I went from Layton City to the Davis County Courthouse and into Ogden trying to find anyone who would listen, trying to tell them this kid had a mental problem and needs help. You just keep running into walls because nobody knows what to do."

Denial is often part of the disease. Injured years ago in a pair of construction accidents, Terrell knew his body was broken. He didn't accept that his mind was in trouble, too.

There was a trespassing charge. The tangents started. Terrell's reality changed in a flash.

Bombs in the ground.

Flash.

Terrell has a cure for cancer—sperm injections. So convinced it would help, Terrell called a New Mexico doctor and later wound up on the steps of the Huntsman Cancer Institute in Salt Lake City.

Flash.

He's convinced he has six children.

Flash.

"It kills you to hear the things they say. He'll get on tangents about people out to get us. I could see him being one of those people the cops shoot."

The medication can halt the flashes of Terrell's changing reality, but Terrell has to take it—and in the right mix.

When his Workers Compensation [payments] ran out, so did his medication.

Terrell could feel the descent.

Knowing that jail had doctors and jail had medicine, he exposed himself to two junior high school girls.

His mother, facing one of the hardest decisions she ever had to make, opted to leave him in jail to help him. (Bryson, "Mental Illness Hijacks Families," C 2)

Words cannot convey the terrible agony suffered day in and day out by Terrell or by his devoted mother.

In a thoughtful and compassionate article on several aspects of mental illness, which appeared some years ago in the *Ensign*, Jan Underwood Pinborough told of a young man whom she called Scott Hausey, though that was not his real name.

Scott . . . was the kind of young man who makes parenting seem easy. He was responsible and religious—an A student who did his homework without being prodded. He enjoyed camping with his parents and six brothers and sisters and planned to be a doctor. Admiring people in his ward would tell Brother and Sister Hausey, "I hope my son will grow up to be like Scott."

Then, about a year into his mission for the Church, Scott became afflicted with a devastating illness. It attacked not his body, but his mind—disordering his thoughts and agitating him so much that he could not finish his mission. Scott began to hear strange voices in his head, voices no one else could hear. He couldn't finish his sentences. At times, he would pace for hours or simply sit in his room and rock.

"I can't describe our emotions when we saw Scott like that," recalls his father. "I thought we'd failed as parents, but we didn't know how."

Scott had a number of counseling sessions and earnestly prayed for the Lord to heal him. Nothing seemed to help. Perhaps, some reasoned, he was possessed by an evil spirit. But Scott was not possessed. He had a serious mental disorder called schizophrenia ("Mental Illness," 51).

Happily, a high councilor in the stake where the Hauseys lived was a physician who recognized the problem and knew of a treatment that could help. With time, patience, medication, and supportive therapy, Scott was able to live a relatively stable life. He married and had a child. He was not cured, but his symptoms were under control, and life again had meaning for him.

In telling these tragic stories—and many others could be added to them—it must be made clear that schizophrenics like Terrell Sorensen and Scott Hausey are much more likely to be the victims rather than the perpetrators of violence. The vast preponderance of violent crimes committed in this or any other nation are not committed by schizophrenics, and, in fact, there is no evidence schizophrenia is associated with increased violence toward others. True, some schizophrenics do commit violent crimes, but the vast majority do not. They retreat into their own private hell.

Recently, two mental disorders afflicting primarily young women have received much public attention. I next turn to them.

Chapter Six

EATING DISORDERS: STARVATION AMIDST PLENTY

A few years ago a girl whom I shall call Melissa was "cruising along" in the ninth grade, her life apparently in good order. Her strong perfectionistic tendencies seemed focused on her school work. She was, and still is, an excellent student. A fellow class member commented to her one day, in an offhand, casual manner, "Melissa, I think you've gained a little weight." Melissa actually was not overweight; already five feet eight inches in height, she weighed about 120 pounds. But she began to obsess over her classmate's casual remark. She began to weigh herself every day. Each day when she looked in the mirror, she recoiled in horror, irrationally believing she was disgustingly, obscenely, grossly obese. She developed an intense fear of being fat and stopped eating normally. She began to eliminate specific food groups one by one from her diet. First, it was no red meat, then no cereals, no vegetables, no milk products. Soon she was eating only a few hundred calories a day, primarily a little white rice and two ounces of grilled chicken breast. She wouldn't let anyone else prepare the food.

83

She was afraid that if anyone else, even her own mother, prepared her food, they'd slip in some fat, unbeknownst to Melissa, and she would get even more grossly overweight than she thought she was.

Melissa's weight began to drop. She developed bruises on her legs, and her hair began to fall out, though she denied any of this was happening. She stopped menstruating; she was pale and fatigued to the point of exhaustion. She became a social recluse who never went out socially, wouldn't talk to friends, and stayed in her own room as much as she could. When she dropped eight pounds in one week, down to under one hundred pounds, her parents had her admitted to the hospital. She stayed there for well over a month as skilled professionals struggled to stabilize her weight, reorder her thinking about herself, and help her to realize what was happening. Finally, she was well enough to go home. But the problem continued. She had to be readmitted to hospital six months later with heart rhythm problems. In effect her body, trying desperately not to die, was cannibalizing her heart muscle.

During the six months she was out of hospital, she had become obsessed with the need to exercise vigorously three times a day, for an hour each time. Though she did not purge herself through vomiting or laxatives (as many anorectics do), she did manage to lose weight by excessively exercising in the face of her ongoing restrictive eating style. As her weight continued to go down, there were fears she would die. She spent more than another month in the hospital, not allowed even to walk to the bathroom, in order to avoid burning any calories on nonessential activities. A liquid diet with exactly measured caloric intake finally stabilized her weight, though the process took several months.

Five years later, Melissa still is struggling, though she is better than she was. She is still convinced she weighs too much, though her total weight and percentage of body fat are well within normal limits. She still exercises vigorously twice a day, and her diet still is rigidly controlled. For several years she would eat each day only two ounces of chicken breast, a spoonful of white rice, a few kernels of corn, a half slice of brown bread, with no butter, of course, and a few bran flakes. Each had to be a specific brand, prepared by herself in a rigidly controlled way and measured to the last gram. If she couldn't get the right brand, she simply refused to eat at all. Her parents spent hours each week searching for the single brand of bran flakes, for example, that she would eat. The extremes to which she went are illustrated by the fact she would *not* use a breath mint, because it contained *one* calorie. A no-cal variety had to be obtained.

She still exhibits bizarre though less extreme eating patterns. For years she would eat only *green* apples, cut up in a certain, specified way. For several months the only fruit she would eat was frozen grapes.

Her obsessive perfectionism still dominates her life. If other students spend ten hours on a project, she will spend a hundred. She continues to be an excellent student and has received numerous scholarship offers at various universities. Her parents hope she will be able to move away from home for her freshman year, but they're not sure what roommates will think of her still immensely rigid food consumption pattern. And what if she's no longer the very top of her class? Will the stress result in her backsliding into worse problems?

ANOREXIA NERVOSA

Melissa exemplifies a person with *anorexia nervosa.* About 90 percent of such patients are female, and the disease is perceived as a female illness (which raises other problems for the relatively few males who are its victims). The usual age of onset is 12–18 years, although the disease may occur later in life. The signs of anorexia are those shown by Melissa. They include the following:

1. Victims of anorexia are chronically unable to sustain their body weight at or above a minimally normal weight for age and height (defined as 85 percent of the expected weight for a person of comparable age and height).

Despite education, encouragement, and severe, often ongoing, medical consequences, the individual resists any effort to increase her weight toward a more normal value. The person will often wear baggy clothes so that others don't notice or comment on her extreme weight loss.

2. Sufferers experience an intense, constant fear of becoming obese.

The person never loses enough weight, in her mind, and feels disgustingly fat even when she has the appearance of a victim from a concentration camp. She always feels she needs to lose more. "You can never be too thin is her motto."

3. Victims have a distorted perception of their body weight or shape.

The person always feels fat; when she looks in the mirror she recoils in horror at what she perceives to be gross obesity or at facial or stomach areas whose shapes she believes indicate that she is overweight.

4. Anorexic females stop menstruating.

The person goes at least three consecutive months without menstruating (amenorrhea) as the body tries to slow its descent to death.

Behaviors associated with these signs of anorexia can include severe restrictions of food intake, with stepwise elimination of first one food group and then another. She pushes her food around on the dinner plate but won't eat. She lies about not feeling well or says she's had a big lunch and doesn't feel hungry. She denies she's ever hungry. To admit her hunger would be a weakness, she thinks.

Searching for a way to sustain her weight at less than 85 percent of normal, the sufferer may begin to exercise fanatically with increasing frequency and intensity, often for several hours per day. When unable to exercise (often due to the injuries sustained from such excess) she becomes frantic with anxiety. Some victims also abuse laxatives, diuretics, and appetite suppressants. Others simply make themselves regurgitate what they have just eaten.

Consequences of these choices include becoming deceitful. As the individual comes to value protecting her anorectic behaviors over maintaining the honesty necessary for close relationships with others, she attempts to hide what is happening to her. To learn what is actually going on, caregivers should rely on objective forms of information, such as measured food intake or random weigh-ins (where the anorectic does not have the opportunity to bulk up by drinking large quantities of water or putting on heavy clothing or secreted weights, all in an effort to disguise the extent of her weight loss).

The person gets progressively more emaciated, fatigued, and depressed. Her ability to concentrate and remember diminishes as her brain begins to suffer from a lack of blood sugar required for proper function.

Unless she is helped, and quickly, the person will simply die from starvation.

Prior to death, there are of course serious medical implications to this self-induced starvation, including heart rhythm disturbances, demineralization of the bones, severe drops in blood pressure, disturbances of hormonal production, kidney failure, and so on. Many of these are signs of starvation. After refeeding, most of the abnormalities usually disappear, although there may be permanent, irremediable damage, most commonly to the bones and heart.

No one knows what causes anorexia. The most prominent theory is that it represents an unconscious attempt to control at least one aspect of one's life—body weight. Probably a complex combination of biological, psychological, and social factors are involved. Some have speculated that anorectic young women fear to grow up, to look like women, and to have women's feelings. The most important practical thing that needs to be done is to begin a weight restoration program immediately, under *very* carefully controlled conditions. Hospitalization often is necessary, since the person's life may be in danger. This must be done in a center that specializes in the treatment of eating disorders: amateur nutritionists are not of much help and may actually do harm. Force-feeding may even be required in emergency situations when death appears imminent and the patient refuses to eat.

Central to the restoration of the patient's recovery from anorexia is the renewing of the spirit. All the force feedings in the world cannot nourish a starving soul. Helping the individual to overcome her aberrant feelings of body image, to find effective ways to express her feelings, and helping her discover and nurture a spiritually based sense of self-worth begins the journey of recovery.

Family therapy also may be indicated, in order to restore honesty in communication and remove unhealthy relationship styles that may be contributing to the disorder. Often by the time a person with anorexia comes to the attention of therapists, her family life may have degenerated into shouting matches over food, often combined with guilt over who's to blame. The more parents shout, order, and remonstrate, the more likely the victim is to refuse, dig in her heels, and obstinately refuse to cooperate. Parents must learn to relinquish control and provide independence, and that's not easy to do, given that they are so frightened about what's happening to a beloved child. Melissa's well-meaning but misinformed grandmother, who kept urging the girl to have some pie, just didn't help. By refusing to eat, Melissa retained control. Without blaming parents or other family members—because to do so just doesn't deal effectively with the problem—all family members must learn how better to talk together in meaningful ways, without feeling guilty or playing the "blame game."

The long-term outlook for patients with anorexia is not terribly optimistic, though most do fairly well in the short run. About one anorectic in five dies from the disorder. Many patients relapse over time and go back to self-starvation and obsessive exercise. Long-term vigilance is required, and both medication and behavioral therapy may be needed. Even then, some patients don't respond well.

The tragic story of Mackenzie Fullmer, as poignantly told by Sarah Jane Weaver in *Church News,* April 27, 2002, is a case in point. Despite prodigious efforts over several years by her family and friends, extensive residential treatment, prayer, fasting and priesthood blessings, Mackenzie slipped further and further away, as her disease took total control of her life. Eventually, she died. "Some stories like this have happy endings," her mother said. "I want people to know that some endings are not happy" ("Mackenzie's Dance," 7).

Unfortunately, many influences in contemporary society reinforce unrealistic ideas about body image in females. There is tremendous pressure for women and girls to maintain an appearance that is sexually attractive to men. Comments such as "You're so lucky to be naturally thin, but I'm just so fat"; the adulation given to emaciated models and movie stars; the constant drumbeat of media emphasis on thinness as a most desirable characteristic—all these combine to teach young girls the wrong lessons about their bodies. Most fashion models, for example, are thinner than 98 percent of American women. Under such pressure, it's no wonder that over 90 percent of college women in a recent survey had attempted to control their weight by dieting. Sad to say, there even are internet chat rooms set up to teach young women how to lose weight for purely cosmetic purposes, with tips on how to deceive their parents and others, utilize effective purging techniques, etc. Such "self-help" misinformation is truly dangerous and may be evil.

There also are disturbing signs that anorexia is beginning to be seen in prepubescent girls, who are beginning to obsess about weight by the time they are eight or nine years of age. Statistics show that more than 80 percent of ten-year-olds are afraid of being fat, and more than half feel better about themselves if they are on a diet. Comments by mothers about their daughters' bodies ("You're so fat, you disgust me"; "Why can't you be thin like Suzy"; or "The boys will never like you, you're so fat") sow the seeds of anorexia that may germinate in the teen years. Such remarks are cruel, stupid, and self-defeating.

Since perfectionism frequently is found in persons suffering from anorexia nervosa, it is appropriate at this point to discuss briefly this common problem. The Latter-day Saints have, if anything, more than their share of perfectionistic tendencies, with all the problems associated with them. Some of us tend to set unattainably high standards for ourselves, standards that no mortal can meet. We tend to think that if we are not perfect, we are failing. We cut ourselves no slack. We castigate ourselves unmercifully because we fall short of unrealistic expectations. We can't forgive ourselves when we stumble and fall, as though life were a test where the passing grade is 100 percent and everything else is a failure.

Perhaps our difficulties with perfectionism arise in part because we misread the Savior's admonition to be perfect, even as He and our Father in Heaven are perfect (see 3 Nephi 12:48). If to be perfect means to be without flaw or blemish, to be totally free of error of any sort, then we are all damned, now and forever. Only one person in all of human history—Jesus Christ, the Lord God Omnipotent—has been perfect. Since "all have sinned, and come short of the glory of God" (Romans 3:23), perfection in that sense is beyond our reach. None of us is perfect, nor, indeed, can we be in mortality. But if to be perfect means to have our flaws and errors eventually removed, to be clean and whole, then we have an achievable, eternal goal to strive for, something that eventually, over the eternities, must be achieved if we are to become as God is. But that will not happen in mortality. In one of his greatest sermons, the King Follett discourse, the Prophet Joseph Smith said:

"When you climb up a ladder, you must begin at the bottom, and ascend step by step, until you arrive at the top; and so it is with the principles of the gospel—you must begin with the first, and go on until you learn all the principles of exaltation. But it will be a great while after you have passed through the veil before you will have learned them. It is not all to be comprehended in this world; it will be a great work to learn our salvation and exaltation even beyond the grave" (*History of the Church*, 6:306–07).

President Joseph Fielding Smith stated the same principle this way:

"Salvation does not come all at once; we are commanded to be perfect even as our Father in Heaven is perfect. It will take us ages to accomplish this end, for there will be greater progress beyond the grave, and it will be there that the faithful will overcome all things, and receive all things, even the fulness of the Father's glory.

"I believe the Lord meant just what he said: that we should be perfect, as our Father in heaven is perfect. That will not come all at once, but line upon line, and precept upon precept, example upon example, and even then not as long as we live in this mortal life, for we will have to go even beyond the grave before we reach that perfection and shall be like God.

"'But here we lay the foundation.'" (*Doctrines of Salvation*, 2:18).

Now, of course, we must strive every day that we live to be better. But we must be realistic in our expectations of ourselves and others. We must not become depressed and discouraged—or perhaps even more, abandon all hope and wallow in the mire of the world as the adversary of truth wishes us to do—if we fall short of perfection.

We must remember, for the sake of our own mental health and that of others around us, that feelings of falling short of eternal goals are natural and the common lot of good people. Elder Neal A. Maxwell has pointed this out: "I speak, not to the slackers in the Kingdom, but to those who carry their own load and more; not to those lulled into false security, but to those buffeted by false insecurity, who, though laboring devotedly in the Kingdom, have recurring feelings of falling forever short . . .

"The first thing to be said of this feeling of inadequacy is that it is normal. . . . Following celestial road signs while in telestial traffic jams is not easy, especially when we are not just moving next door—or even across town" ("Notwithstanding My Weakness," 12).

Above all else, we must grow to understand, not just with our intellects but in our hearts, that you don't have to be perfect to be loved or to be worthy of love. How tragic it is when someone goes through life without learning that lesson. A dying man said to Rabbi Harold S. Kushner: "When I was young, I thought I had to be perfect for people to love me. I thought if I ever did something wrong, their love would be withdrawn. So every time I did something wrong, I would make excuses, I would lie, I would try to find someone else to blame. I didn't realize what an unpleasant person I became when I acted that way. I thought it was my imperfection, not my defensiveness, that turned people off. But lying here in the hospital—sick and cranky and dying, but feeling God's presence in the doctors and nurses who try to help me, in the friends and family who come to visit me—I've finally learned that you don't have to be perfect to be worth loving. I only wish I had known that sooner" ("You Don't Have to Be Perfect").

The devilish misunderstandings about the doctrine that you have to be perfect are given unwarranted credence by the world in which we live—a world which leads women to think they can never be as pretty or as glamorous as models or movie stars. Our world teaches women that their worth as a person is dependent on how they look, that the only way to be good and successful is to be thin and pretty. It is a world that teaches men they can never earn enough, and must never lose, as though the team that loses the World Series of baseball should hang its head in shame.

Parents who value the mental health of their children must help them to realize that their parents' love is enduring. Regardless of what happens, that love must always be there. That assurance is especially important for those who are suffering mental illness, with the added burden it brings, the almost overwhelming feelings of unworthiness that accompany it. Enduring love, compassion, and acceptance, along with the feeling that burdens are shared and not the exclusive trial of a lone sufferer, are essential if healing is to occur. Insofar as eating disorders are concerned, it is important for families to foster an environment in the home that does not reinforce the false idea that you must excel to be worthy of love, and that you can't be good unless you're thin.

Finally, it cannot be overemphasized that ultimately it is up to the victim of anorexia to decide whether she will live or die, succumb or survive. No real progress can be made until the victim herself decides she must change. Many such young women have poor self-images and much anxiety in their lives. Until those faulty perceptions are changed, victims will continue to struggle. For example, Mackenzie Fullmer, whose losing battle with eating disorders was mentioned briefly previously, had an older sister, Adrie, who almost succumbed herself but finally was able to break away from the monster that threatened to take her life.

BULIMIA

Another eating disorder, which unfortunately, like anorexia, can become life threatening, is *bulimia*. Diana, Princess of Wales, reportedly was bulimic, as are many high-school- and college-aged women. Persons with bulimia (almost all are women) suffer from binge eating, followed by purging. Binge eating, by definition, is not just having another slice of cake, it's eating the whole cake, plus a quart of high-fat gourmet ice

95

cream. Bulimics feel a lack of control over their eating during these recurring episodes. Having consumed such tremendous amounts of food, the bulimic feels compelled to get rid of it in order to not gain weight. Most commonly this is done by self-induced vomiting. Alternatively, or at other times additionally, bulimic individuals often misuse laxatives, enemas, diuretics, or weight loss medications. Many fast excessively. Excessive physical exercise is common in an attempt to balance out the episodic bingeing. These troublesome behaviors occur on average at least twice a week for a period of at least three months. Like the anorexic, the bulimic renders harsh self-evaluations of her body's shape and weight. She too sees her body through a distorted perspective. Nevertheless, that perspective is what she holds to be true, even in the face of such medical consequences as severe acid burns in her throat and mouth (from vomiting), progressive deterioration of her teeth and gums, and profound episodes of cardiac-driven chest pains (often the early warning of the cardiac collapse that takes the life of so many afflicted with this disorder).

Persons with bulimia often have other psychiatric conditions, such as depression or obsessive-compulsive disorder (OCD). They often feel very anxious just before they binge. They commonly suffer from immense self-hatred, such that if they ever lose control over what they eat, even a little, by eating, let's say, a single doughnut, they feel terrible about themselves: "I'm just horrible. I can't control what I eat. I've no will-power. I'm just no good. I might as well eat the whole dozen doughnuts, and a quart of ice cream, too."

Persons with bulimia often also abuse alcohol or other drugs, perhaps to relieve their feelings of self-loathing, guilt, depression, or anxiety. Those with mild forms of bulimia may benefit from behavioral therapy, but severe cases may require medication in addition, particularly some of the newer anti-depressants. Since patients with bulimia not uncommonly also suffer from depression or OCD, drugs that treat those prob-lems also may be of value in treating bulimia. Relapses of persons with bulimia are common.

Suicide is a real threat in the lives of many people who are mentally ill. Difficult and painful though the topic is to talk about, it deserves discussion.

Chapter Seven

THE DARK
SPECTER OF SUICIDE

A few years ago a man I know well was asked to speak at the funeral of a young wife and mother who had killed herself. She had been married for time and eternity to a fine priesthood holder, had several young children, was multi-talented, and on the surface had a great life ahead of her and everything to live for. But she became depressed after the birth of her last child and slowly slipped deeper and deeper into a terrible gulf of blackness and despair. Family and friends recognized she was struggling somewhat but thought it was only temporary and that she'd soon be her old self again. No one, including her faithful husband, who was serving as a bishop at the time, really understood the depths of her hopelessness and depression. Finally, unable to bear the terrible pain and feelings of utter sadness, she unwisely took her own life.

This tragedy, sadly, is repeated over and over again in severely depressed persons of both sexes, one in six of whom kill themselves. More than 30,000 people in the United States alone kill themselves each year, and it is estimated by the World

Health Organization that approximately one million people worldwide commit suicide annually. The number of suicides among those who suffer from bipolar disorder, in which periods of deep depression alternate with episodes of agitated euphoria, may be as high as one in four sufferers. It is clear that depression is a potentially fatal disease and that the possibility of suicide in depressed persons should always be considered and never underestimated.

The man asked to speak at the funeral was himself a senior Church leader, who knew something about the seriousness of taking an innocent life. He understood as well the grief felt by the husband, children, parents, and friends of the dead woman. He sensed that each of them also bore deep feelings of guilt over what had happened. "If only I'd paid more attention," her husband said, through his tears. "What happens to our eternal marriage? I suppose I've lost her forever." And her parents sobbed, "What did we do wrong in raising her?" The children felt that Mommy had gone away because of something they'd done or said. In their childish sorrow, they blamed themselves.

The Church leader knew that it is never helpful (and, in this instance, it was certainly not true) to say that those around the dead woman were responsible for the tragic act that ended her life. All had done the best they could. None had wanted this to happen. None had aided it. But the Church leader knew that if needed healing was to occur in the survivors, he would have to address the problem of suicide head-on. He couldn't condone what had been done, but at the same time he desperately wanted to lift and comfort those left behind. In a very real way they were victims, too. While he knew that he must be loving and kind, the Church leader recognized that his first responsibility was to be faithful to the teachings of the Church. He was familiar with President Boyd K. Packer's wise comment: "The study of the doctrines of the gospel will improve behavior quicker than a study of behavior will improve behavior" ("Little Children," 18). He began to read what the prophets have said on the matter of suicide. President Spencer W. Kimball put it bluntly: "It is a terrible criminal act for a person to go out and shorten his life by suicide" (*Teachings of Spencer W. Kimball*, 187). But President Kimball qualified that indictment, saying: "To commit suicide is a sin *if one is normal in his thinking*" (ibid., 187; emphasis added).

Elder George Q. Cannon, then a member of the First Presidency, spoke many years ago about the seriousness of suicide. He said: "Man did not create himself. He did not furnish his spirit with a human dwelling place. It is God who created man, both body and spirit. Man has no right, therefore, to destroy that which he had no agency in creating. They who do so are guilty of murder, self-murder it is true, but they are no more justified in killing themselves than they are in killing others. What difference of punishment there is for the two crimes, I do not know; but it is clear that no one can destroy so precious a gift as that of life without incurring a severe penalty" (*Gospel Truth*, 25).

The Church leader bowed his head in sorrow: was there no room for hope? The words *sin, crime,* and *murder* tumbled over and over in his mind. But then he read further. Elder Bruce R. McConkie of the Quorum of the Twelve Apostles also stressed the serious nature of suicide, but at the same time implied that

101

we should be slow to judge motives, abilities, thoughts, and intentions:

"Suicide consists in the voluntary and intentional taking of one's own life, particularly where the person involved is accountable and has a sound mind. Mortal life is a gift of God; it comes according to the divine will, is appointed to endure for such time as Deity decrees, and is designed to serve as the chief testing period of man's eternal existence. It is the probationary state or time during which man is tried and tested physically, spiritually, and mentally. No man has the right to run away from these tests, no matter how severe they may be, by taking his own life. Obviously persons subject to great stresses may lose control of themselves and become mentally clouded to the point that they are no longer accountable for their acts. Such are not to be condemned for taking their own lives. It should also be remembered that judgment is the Lord's; he knows the thoughts, intents, and abilities of men; and he in his infinite wisdom will make all things right in due course" (*Mormon Doctrine*, 771).

Perhaps, the Church leader began to realize, it is necessary in considering this matter, while giving full weight to the seriousness of taking one's own life, to recognize also the likelihood that those who do so while in the depths of mental illness may not be fully accountable for their acts. Was thinking along the lines of diminished accountability in the mentally ill just a cop-out, he wondered? No, he concluded, it wasn't. He knew, from experience in his own family, that the pain and suffering from depression, for example, is well-nigh impossible to describe. It perhaps exceeds any suffering of physical origin. It seems never-ending. It is compounded by the terrible, almost overwhelming feelings of abandonment, anguish, and hope-lessness that accompany it.

The Church leader remembered when he himself had had serious surgery. The pain was intense, but medication eased it, and in just a few days the pain subsided. Each new day, he had had reason to believe, would be better, more pain-free than the last. But, he wondered, how would I have reacted, would I have been so resolute, if the pain had gone on and on and never ended? And even more, would I have coped well if at the same time I'd been consumed with the overwhelming feeling that God had abandoned me, that nothing mattered, that no one could help, and that there was no hope for me now or in eternity? Those thoughts sobered and humbled the Church leader. He felt less judgmental. Perhaps, he thought, he should be slow to judge what might have been going through the mind of someone who had committed suicide while depressed or otherwise mentally ill. We can never really know in this life: the only mortal witness is dead. Perhaps we should leave it up to God to judge. He and only He knows all the facts.

Peace came into the Church leader's heart as he realized the central truth of what Church leaders have taught: leave the judgment to God. Only He can render a just and perfect judgment. Only He recognizes differences in intent and circum-stances. Only He knows if what happened was a pitiful call for help that went too long unheeded. Only He knows if the person involved was capable of fully understanding the seriousness and finality of his or her actions. Only He understands the full impact of chemical abnormalities in the brain and how they might affect behavior, self-control, and the ability to think rationally. Only He can unravel the tangled knot consisting of both genetic predisposition and environmental stress.

The Church leader also remembered the words of Elder Marion D. Hanks, who has written with his characteristic sensitivity and compassion about a boy who had committed suicide. In an address given at Brigham Young University on 26 August 1976, Elder Hanks said:

"Perhaps I should not mention without time and proper occasion to discuss it fully the sobering experience of sitting with the family and speaking at the services of the boy who took his own life. But I am impressed to share with you the strong assurance that came and was expressed: he is in the loving care of the Holy One of Israel, who stands at the gate and 'employeth no servant there'—that Holy One who took not upon himself 'the nature of angels; but . . . the seed of Abraham' in order that He might have 'the feeling of our infirmities.' He has 'descended below' the fiercest of our sufferings. Better than anyone else in all of history, He understands what it means to feel all alone. It was He who on the cross cried out, 'My God, my God, why hast thou forsaken me?'" (*Bread upon the Waters,* 84).

A snatch of words from a favorite hymn echoed in the Church leader's mind: "Judge not, that ye be not judged, Was the counsel Jesus gave; Measure given, large or grudged, Just the same you must receive" (*Hymns,* no. 273). These words, he knew, reflected those of the Savior Himself: "Judge not, that ye be not judged. For with what judgment ye judge, ye shall be judged: and with what measure ye mete, it shall be measured to you again" (Matthew 7:1).

Now it was possible for the Church leader to draw a conclusion from his reading and pondering: suicide is a sin, a serious one, but the Lord will not judge the person who commits that sin strictly on the act alone. He will consider all the circumstances involved, perhaps particularly the accountability of the person concerned. Nothing in that, however, gives license to deny individual responsibility or to excuse the commission of sin. We must be very careful not to avoid responsibility by saying, "The devil made me do it," or "I couldn't help myself." We must ever strive to follow the Savior and His teachings. Help, if needed, must be sought and accepted before the mind becomes so clouded that accountability may seriously be questioned. President Spencer W. Kimball's wise comments bear repetition:

"A minister acquaintance of mine, whom I knew rather well, was found by his wife hanging in the attic from the rafters. His thoughts had taken his life. He had become morose and despondent for two or more years. Certainly he had not come to suicide in a moment, for he had been a happy, pleasant person as I had known him. It must have been a long decline, ever steeper, controllable by him at first and perhaps out of hand as he neared the end of the trail. No one in his 'right mind,' and especially if he has an understanding of the gospel, will permit himself to arrive at this 'point of no return' (*Teachings of Spencer W. Kimball,* 188).

RECOGNIZING THE WARNING SIGNS OF SUICIDE

Prevention—an ounce of which truly is worth more than a pound of cure—is particularly important with regard to

105

suicide, for rather obvious reasons. Before we discuss the warning signs it is necessary to note some of the distressing facts about this terrible tragedy. They include the following:

- Women attempt suicide three to four times more often than men, but men are four times as likely as women to be successful in their attempts to kill themselves, primarily because of the methods chosen.
- In the United States, suicide is the third leading cause of death among young people aged 15–24.
- For more than ten years, 15- to 34-year-old males in Utah have had suicide rates higher than those seen nationally. More than half of those who kill themselves do so at home.
- In a detailed analysis of records from the Utah State Department of Health, Dr. Sterling C. Hilton and his colleagues noted that the suicide rate among *less*-active members of The Church of Jesus Christ of Latter-day Saints, aged 25–29, was seven times higher than among their *active* Church peers. Nationally, the suicide rate among 20- to 34-year-old males was 2.5–3 times *higher* than among active Latter-day Saints (Hilton et. al., "Suicide Rates and Religious Commitment," 413–19).

These data show conclusively that a low level of religious commitment is a risk factor for suicide. *Active* members of The Church of Jesus Christ of Latter-day Saints, and perhaps of other churches as well, are less likely to commit suicide than the public in general.

- The rate of suicide goes up with age, particularly with men over age 65, and is highest for white men over 85.

• Four of five people who commit suicide have made at least one previous attempt: there are from 8–25 attempted suicides for one completion.

What, then, are some of the clues and danger signals that indicate someone may be at risk for suicide? They include the following, although it must be noted there is no *sure* way to predict if and when someone will attempt suicide:

1. Depression. Studies indicate that a high percentage of suicides occur within the context of mental illness and usually in response to multiple stressors. Depression is the most common factor in suicide. As noted in chapter 4, signs of depression include withdrawal from social interaction; changes in appetite, weight, sleep patterns, physical activity, and energy level; intense feelings of worthlessness; feelings that the individual is guilty of something or other and deserves to be punished; loss of interest in personal appearance; repeated "crying jags"; difficulty in thinking, concentrating, and making decisions; and recurring thoughts of death and suicide. A definitive diagnosis and subsequent treatment of depression should not be attempted by lay persons but is best left in the hands of competent mental health professionals.

2. Substance abuse. Persons suffering the pain of depression or other mental illness may seek relief by taking alcohol or other mood-altering drugs. The resulting loss of the person's ability to control his or her impulses and deterioration in judgment simply increases the likelihood he or she may act on the self-destructive thoughts and impulses that can accompany many forms of severe mental illness.

3. Extreme stress. Stressful life events, such as divorce or marital separation; the death of a spouse, child, or other loved one; rejection by family or friends; loss of employment; fear of public exposure of shameful behavior; or financial ruin can trigger a desire to "end it all."

4. Illness. A person may seek ultimate relief from terminal, extremely painful, or debilitating illness.

5. Ruined relationships. Dysfunctional family relationships, including physical or sexual abuse or other family violence, may precipitate thoughts of suicide.

6. Anger and hostility. Persons with feelings of intense hostility, especially males, may turn anger inward upon themselves if they lack adequate outlets for their rage.

7. Loneliness. The loneliness of living alone, especially as experienced by elderly men, is sometimes a factor.

8. Family history of suicide. Prior suicide attempts, or suicide by a family member, perhaps a parent or sibling, need to be considered in evaluating a person's vulnerability.

9. Verbal warnings. Most people who consider suicide give verbal warnings such as, "I'm going to end it all"; "I don't want to be a burden"; "I can't stand it any longer"; or "People would be better off without me." An estimated 80 percent of people who commit suicide talk about it beforehand. *Always take verbal warnings seriously, even those uttered in seeming jest, and investigate them promptly.*

10. Preparation for death. Attention should be paid if an individual who has given other clues and signals begins putting his or her affairs in order, acquires a firearm or other means of destruction, makes a will, or discusses insurance policies, etc., particularly if such events are followed by a heightened attitude of well-being. For example, one man signaled his preparation for imminent death by purchasing a rope with which to hang himself and then letting others know he had done so. Though he was deadly serious in what he did, nevertheless, as with most people who contemplate suicide, he did not really want to die. He wanted to resolve his problems and lead a normal life but didn't know how to do so.

11. Preoccupation with firearms. This is an especially chilling indicator, particularly if the person has previously shown little interest in guns.

SOME HELPFUL ADVICE FOR LOVED ONES

Spouses, parents, and other family members should talk openly to those whose behavior indicates they are at risk for suicide. They should not be afraid to ask the person if he is thinking about committing suicide. Talking openly, frankly, and nonjudgmentally about suicidal thoughts and feelings will not plant the idea in the head of the person concerned. Count on it: *that idea is already there.* Frank discussion will, in fact, decrease the likelihood of suicide, by letting the person know he is taken seriously, that the feelings involved are not shameful, and that others care deeply about the individual and do not condemn him.

Ask whether a method for committing suicide has been considered and if specific plans have been made. Try to do so in a calm, nonthreatening, and nonjudgmental way. Do not preach or list reasons why the person should not commit suicide. Don't argue with the individual.

Never dismiss a suicidal threat or make light of it. Persons contemplating suicide need attention, not dismissal. Assume they mean what they say.

Never try to shock or challenge the person by saying, "Oh, go ahead and do it" or "All you ever do is talk," or "You're just bluffing, as usual." That's just an invitation for him to carry out the threat. Patiently listen to the sorrows and woes of the person involved, even if you've heard them umpteen times already. Remember that most suicidal persons do not really want to die—they want help.

Parents of adolescents should be aware that suicide is the third leading cause of death among teenagers. Many of the same risk factors that apply to the general population also apply to adolescents. Many young people who contemplate suicide have not fully thought through the finality of the act and may have developed romanticized fantasies about it. A case in point: a teenage boy, in what appears to have been primarily an impulsive, spur-of-the-moment act, killed himself, in the family home, with his father's hunting rifle. No one—not parents, siblings, or friends—had the slightest idea the boy was planning anything other than his normal Saturday night activities, and he was not seriously depressed, so far as anyone knew.

Parents should avoid describing methods of suicide or discussing risk factors with teenagers. Such discussions may serve only to legitimatize suicide as the way out of problems. Teaching youth the doctrines of the gospel will help them to solve their problems in the Lord's way. Remember President Packer's counsel mentioned earlier: "The study of the doctrines of the gospel will improve behavior quicker than a study of behavior will improve behavior."

Teenagers—and adults too, for that matter—need to learn the doctrine of restoration: the fact is that the feelings, attitudes, and attributes we develop in this world will be carried with us into the next. As the Nephite prophet Amulek said, "That same spirit which doth possess your bodies at the time that ye go out of this life, that same spirit will have power to possess your body in that eternal world" (Alma 34:34). Alma's advice to his son Corianton bears on the same theme:

"And now, my son, all men that are in a state of nature, or I would say, in a carnal state, are in the gall of bitterness and the bonds of iniquity; they are without God in the world, and they have gone contrary to the nature of God; therefore, they are in a state contrary to the nature of happiness. And now behold, is the meaning of the word restoration to take a thing of a natural state and place it in an unnatural state, or to place it in a state opposite to its nature? O, my son, this is not the case; but the meaning of the word restoration is to bring back again evil for evil, or carnal for carnal, or devilish for devilish—good for that which is good; righteous for that which is righteous; just for that which is just; merciful for that which is merciful" (Alma 41:11–13).

In other words, those who believe mistakenly that killing themselves will solve all their problems are quite simply wrong.

Parents of teenagers who are at risk for suicidal behavior should enlist the help of Church leaders. There is no substitute for the counsel of a wise bishop, who also may encourage the young person involved to seek professional help.

111

Family members should be alert for signs of depression and other risk factors for suicide in aging parents or other aging relatives. Factors such as depression, increasing age, being male, isolation, physical illness, and loss of a spouse through death or divorce all increase the risk of suicide. Again, talking frankly about potential problems is the best way to prevent them from happening. It may be advisable to encourage aged parents and other relatives to get appropriate help from medical and mental health professionals. A wise bishop can be of invaluable assistance both in counseling and in marshaling Church and community resources to assist older adults as needed.

TEARS AND SORROW, THE AFTERMATH OF SUICIDE

Suicide inevitably leaves in its wake survivors caught in a web of grief and guilt. Grief at the loss of a loved one; anger directed toward the person who died, and perhaps toward God, who did not stop the tragedy from happening; and guilt because of unresolved relationship problems or perceived personal failure to prevent the tragedy combine to create a constellation of turmoil that may last for years. Indeed, it is possible that, in terms of the suffering involved, the survivors carry a heavier burden than the one who died. For one thing, family, friends, and others don't know what to say to the survivors, nor how to act toward them. The normal diffidence, hesitancy, and uncertainty associated with dealing with death and sorrow are accentuated by the stigma, prejudice, and general lack of knowledge about suicide. What survivors need more than anything else is love and nonjudgmental acceptance. As Alma the

Elder said to those gathered at the waters of Mormon, we must be "willing to bear one another's burdens, that they may be light; . . . [and] to mourn with those that mourn; yea, and comfort those that stand in need of comfort" (Mosiah 18:8–9). Taking a casserole to the grieving survivors as an expression of shared sorrow is important, to be sure, but even more important may be a simple, "I'm so sorry," followed by a sincere expression of nonjudgmental love for everyone involved—the bereaved and the primary victim alike.

Suicide survivors can expect to go through the various stages of grief as outlined by Elisabeth Kübler-Ross in her book *On Death and Dying.* These include denial and shock; anger and blame; guilt and bargaining; depression and loneliness; and finally acceptance. The rate of progression through these stages of grieving will vary from person to person, but all must be undergone and endured, even if it takes years to do so. Otherwise, complete healing cannot occur. Counsel from Church leaders and perhaps from mental health professionals may be necessary to assist in this process.

One of the first issues that survivors must face is the funeral. The *Church Handbook of Instructions* indicates that "the family, in consultation with the bishop, determines the place and nature of a funeral service for a person who has died under such circumstances [i.e., by suicide]. Church facilities may be used." It is important that survivors understand "the body of a person who has committed suicide is not dishonored. If the person has been endowed and otherwise is in good standing with the Church, the body may be buried in temple clothes" (Sullivan, "Suicide," 1422).

Children whose sibling or parent has committed suicide often are terribly confused, frightened, and deeply troubled. They may believe, erroneously, that they in some way are at fault. They may worry that someone else in the family, perhaps they themselves, will die soon. They may have difficulty sleeping, become clingy and weepy, lose weight, have trouble at school, withdraw from others; in short, they may become deeply depressed themselves. They should be provided with accurate and honest information, consistent of course with their level of understanding. They should be encouraged to ask questions and discuss their feelings openly with trusted family members and Church leaders. They must be assured, repeatedly if necessary, that the suicide was not their fault. They should be assured of God's love for them, that things will get better, and that others will be there to protect and care for them. They should be reminded of God's love for *all* His children.

Ultimately, the only way to heal after the death of a loved one from suicide is to leave the matter in God's hands. As Elder M. Russell Ballard has said, "Only our Father in Heaven knows the full answer to the questions our hearts ask regarding those who take their own lives." He continues: "As I think about the worry and agony of those whose loved one has taken his or her own life, I find deep comfort and faith in the Lord's promise and blessing to us who remain in mortality: 'Peace I leave with you, my peace I give unto you: not as the world giveth, give I unto you. Let not your heart be troubled, neither let it be afraid' (John 14:27)" ("Suicide," 9).

Where, then, can we turn for that peace we so desperately need? The final chapter presents my views on this most important matter.

Chapter Eight

NOT MY WILL,
BUT THINE, BE DONE

It will have become apparent that the emotional, spiritual, and physical toll from mental disease is horrendous. It exceeds the ability of words to describe. The tsunami of suffering extends outward from the victim to engulf family members, friends, Church associates, and fellow workers. All involved struggle to try to make sense out of what is going on. Dreams are discarded, hopes dashed. Panic, sorrow, and a sense of hopelessness can pervade every waking moment.

Yet in the midst of all the pain and sorrow there is hope. First of all, during the last four decades, great advances have been made in the field of psychopharmacology. For the first time in human history potent new drugs have had major success in treating victims with a broad variety of mental disorders. True, they are not perfect, as I have said. They are not yet the "silver bullet" longed for by researchers and physicians, which will zero in on the problem, eliminating it while leaving the rest of the body unaffected. Unwanted side effects can still be troublesome but in most instances are controllable. Some patients just don't respond adequately to available therapy. For example, statistics show that roughly 20 percent of those being treated for depression do not respond at all to drug therapy. But help is on the way. There is great hope, and it is generally acknowledged, that biological and medical research will lead, over time, to new and improved therapeutic interventions for mental disorders. New medications, more specific in their effect and free of the deleterious side effects that reduce the value of much of what is available today, can be expected. Many, indeed, already are in the research and development pipeline.

Further, as our knowledge of how the brain works increases—and don't forget that organ has been called the most complicated thing in the universe—the ingenuity of man will lead us to better therapy for mental illness. I am sure of that. I also firmly believe God guides the hands of those who strive to better the lot of their fellowmen in this area of need and in all others.

The value of nonmedicinal therapies continues. Proper diet, avoidance of potentially addictive substances and behaviors, moderation from various excesses, regular physical exercise, and attention to discovering and implementing a gospel-centered understanding of who we are within this earthly experience remain staples to sound mental health. Skilled talk therapy, which assists sufferers to understand why they think as they do and helps them to overcome unhealthy or aberrant thoughts, provides a benefit that medication alone cannot afford. To overcome or manage mental illness, we must exert all the inner strength we can muster while utilizing all the biological tools skilled health professionals can prescribe.

There is hope, too, that the age-old prejudice and bigotry against those who suffer from mental illness will decrease over time, as ignorance gives way to knowledge and more people come to understand no one is immune from mental disease. Indeed, some of that needed increase in compassion already is occurring. I pray that the pace of change in this area will increase, as people come to understand that much of mental illness is the brain equivalent of biological disorders occurring elsewhere in the body. I long for the day when we become part of a Zion people, who will live together in full acceptance of each other, with no dissension or unkindness, each serving as his or her brother's keeper, not out of duty but out of love.

But beyond the hopes for tomorrow, no matter how firm they may be, what about today? Pain and patience are uneasy partners. Where suffering is involved, there is little concern about what may happen in the future, no matter how promising. The only concern is for relief *now,* in the present. What can be done today to lift the heavy burdens of sorrow, fear, and hopelessness, especially among those sufferers for whom nothing seems to work particularly well, whose days are a long progression of gray emptiness, punctuated by flashes of acute torment? Every sufferer longs to be healed, or for a beloved family member or friend to be healed. Each longs for brighter days and renewed hope, with no more tears and no more turmoil. But sometimes prayers are not answered as we had hoped so fervently they would be answered. Sometimes dramatic miracles do not occur. Sometimes the victim, along with those around him or her, is left to tread the winepress alone. Sometimes all that can be done is to endure, to hang on, to do one's best amid tears and turmoil, and to struggle each day just to survive. What then?

The answer, I believe, lies in a single line of scripture. When Mary, the virgin mother-to-be of Jesus, was told by the angel that she would bring forth a son named Jesus, "the Son of the Highest," she exclaimed: "*Be it unto me according to thy word*" (Luke 1:31–32, 38; emphasis added). Even though at that stage of her experience she did not fully understand her glorious destiny, Mary was humbly submissive, fully obedient. If we are to survive the trials of life with our faith intact, there is, quite simply, no other answer: "Not as I will, but as thou wilt" (Matthew 26:39) must be our motto. Only through submissiveness can we find lasting peace.

To believe that, and more importantly, to live it, requires great faith, often more than we knew we had. Oh, that our faith might be as that of the three young Israelites, Shadrach, Meshach, and Abed-nego. As they were about to be thrown into a fiery furnace, heated so hot that "the flame of the fire" devoured their keepers, the young men proclaimed their faith: "If it be so, our God whom we serve is able to deliver us from the burning fiery furnace, and he will deliver us out of thine hand, O King." Then these words of calm assurance: "*But if not*, be it known unto thee, O King, that we will not serve thy gods, nor worship the golden image which thou hast set up" (Daniel 3:17–18; emphasis added). Even when faced with the possibility God would not choose to rescue them from a horrible death, the three faithful young men were resolute: they *would not* worship the heathen gods of Nebuchadnezzar, come what may. So it must be with us: we may have to endure trials more horrendous than we think possible. There are times we simply must "be still, and know that [He is] God" (Psalm 46:10). We are reminded, "My people must be tried in all things, that they may be prepared to receive the glory that I have for them, even the glory of Zion; and he that will not bear chastisement is not worthy of my kingdom" (D&C 136:31). This is difficult, wintry doctrine, but true.

Patience also is required of us—a patient endurance, the "patience of hope" (1 Thessalonians 1:3), even when the burden is galling. Indeed, God "trieth [our] patience and [our] faith. Nevertheless—whosoever putteth his trust in him the same shall be lifted up at the last day" (Mosiah 23:21–22). In times of great travail, Alma learned that God will "ease the burdens which are put upon your shoulders, that even you cannot feel them upon your backs" (Mosiah 24:14). Thus the Lord counsels that we are to "be patient in long-suffering and afflictions, . . . and I will make an instrument of thee in my hands unto the salvation of many souls" (Alma 17:11). "Bear with patience thine afflictions, and I will give unto you success" (Alma 26:27).

But patience can wear thin unless we grow to trust in God and His plans for us and have faith that sometime—whether in this world or the next—all will be made right, for "he careth for [us]" (1 Peter 5:7). President Brigham Young put it wisely:

"When the Latter-day Saints make up their minds to endure, for the Kingdom of God's sake, whatsoever shall come, whether poverty or riches, whether sickness or to be driven by mobs, they will say it is all right, and will honor the hand of the Lord in it, and in all things, and serve Him to the end of their lives, according to the best of their ability, God being their helper. If you have not made up your minds for this, the quicker you do so the better" (*Journal of Discourses,* 1:338).

But what *are* God's plans for us? They center on and have their foundation firmly anchored in Jesus' atonement and resurrection. He and He alone is our Advocate with the Father. He showed the way. We can teach Him nothing about suffering. He has testified of the pain He endured in purchasing our sins and atoning for our shortcomings: "Which suffering caused myself, even God, the greatest of all, to tremble because of pain, and to bleed at every pore, and to suffer both body and spirit—and would that I might not drink the bitter cup, and shrink—Nevertheless, glory be to the Father, and I partook and finished my preparations unto the children of men" (D&C 19:18–19). Christ's incomprehensible suffering permits Him to fully empathize with ours.

Jesus, who suffered more than mortals can comprehend, who knew the crushing burden of the sins of the world, came to earth not to end all suffering, but to end the *needless* suffering brought on by sin and to teach us that suffering need not be in vain. Through the infinite grace of His atonement, He will help us find the ability to endure. Wondrous promises of eternal joy are ours if we do so. His empathy is perfect, His understanding full and complete!

Since Christ and His Father are one in attributes and perfection, we can plead with the Father, in the name of the Son, about our trials and pain. He too understands perfectly. Such pleading is not cowardice or even weakness, but an evidence of our faith in and our total dependence on the God who loves us.

Though Christ's atonement brings a universal resurrection to all of humankind—"For as in Adam all die, even so in Christ shall all be made alive" (1 Corinthians 15:22)—the second part of His atonement, the gift of eternal life, is reserved for the faithful. To that extent, then, we must "work out our salvation." As Elder Neal A. Maxwell has said, from the wisdom of his own experience, "Suffering accounts for some of the sweat that goes with the process of working out our salvation" (*One More Strain of Praise,* 7). That suffering may be long or short. If it teaches us to be submissive and humble, we will have learned one of eternity's greatest lessons. Of one thing we can be sure: the price of discipleship is and ever will be tutorial suffering. There are no exceptions to that rule, no cheap and easy way to "take up [our] cross and follow [Him]" (Mark 10:21). There may well be variations in suffering, both as to time and intensity, but there are no exceptions. It is learning to endure whatever mortality brings us that is the key that opens the door leading to celestial halls.

Sufferers of mental illness know from experience how hard it is to appreciate and cultivate the sunny side of life while being battered by a hurricane of darkness and despair. It is hard to keep in mind a glorious tomorrow beyond the veil where there will be no tears or sorrow, no broken dreams, no times when a person is trying with all her strength to just hang on, to make it through another dreary, painful day. Yet Jesus, the Great Exemplar, who always points the way for us, declared: "Be of good cheer" (John 16:33). "I will lead you along," He assures us. "The kingdom is yours and the blessings thereof are yours, and the riches of eternity are yours" (D&C 78:18). No matter if our path be strewn with thorns, no matter how hard and onerous the struggle through mists of disappointment, no matter though we be bowed with care and pain, He will guide us. He will be our leader, if we in humility will follow Him: "Be thou humble; and the Lord thy God shall lead thee by the hand, and give thee answer to thy prayers" (D&C 112:10). To take Him by the hand requires us to acknowledge that without Him we are as lost children, weak and incapable of rescuing ourselves and unable to find our way home again. We need not be ashamed or even embarrassed to show Him our weakness. After all, He knows us perfectly! Furthermore, "the Lord God showeth us our weakness that we may know that it is by his grace, and his great condescensions unto the children of men, that we have power to do these things" (Jacob 4:7). Additionally, "I give unto men weakness that they may be humble; and my grace is sufficient for all men that humble themselves before me; for if they humble themselves before me, and have faith in me, then will I make weak things become strong unto them" (Ether 12:27).

One of the problems we struggle against in our efforts to know God's purpose for us is the myopia of mortality. We simply cannot see clearly beyond the veil that separates this world from the next. Our mortal experience, though a vital part of our eternal journey, is small-scale at best, a grain of sand on the vast seashore of eternity. We lack the perspective and sense of proportion required to see things "as they really are." Will Durant, the famous historian, wrote of our need for that perspective: "to know that the little things are little, and the big things big, before it is too late; we want to see things now as they seem forever—'in the light of eternity'" (*Story of Philosophy,* 1).

Despite that need to see things in "the light of eternity" we, in our spiritual immaturity, see as "through a glass, darkly." "But when that which is perfect is come, then that which is in part shall be done away. Then [shall we see] face to face: now [we] know in part; but then shall [we] know even as also [we are] known" (1 Corinthians 13:10, 12).

Having said that, I emphasize that we at times do sense our eternal nature and eternal destiny. As Lucy Maud Montgomery wrote: "It has always seemed to me, ever since early childhood, amid all the commonplaces of life, I was very near to a kingdom of ideal beauty. Between it and me hung only a thin veil. I could never draw it quite aside, but sometimes a wind fluttered it and I caught a glimpse of the enchanting realm beyond—only a glimpse—but those glimpses have always made life worthwhile" (Introduction to *Anne of Green Gables,* xiii-xiv). Perhaps the poet Wordsworth had similar intimations:

> Our birth is but a sleep and a forgetting:
> The Soul that rises with us, our life's Star,
> Hath had elsewhere its setting,
> And cometh from afar:
> Not in entire forgetfulness,
> And not in utter nakedness,
> But trailing clouds of glory do we come
> From God, who is our home.
> (*Oxford Dictionary of Quotations*, 579).

But in general, the veil between this life and the next is parted only at death. Thus, we fail to understand that whatever we have to undergo on earth, no matter how stern our mortal trials, they, too, will pass away, and the time will come when "God shall wipe away all tears from [our] eyes; and there shall be no more death, neither sorrow, nor crying, neither shall there be any more pain: for the former things are passed away" (Revelation 21:4).

But how can we communicate with God, how can we plead with Him to ease our pain and dry our tears, when, if we pray, the heavens are as brass, and it seems as though God is forever separated from us? How do we pray when our despair is so deep and black that we can't think the thoughts, far less speak the words? How do we communicate when the Spirit seems a stranger to us?

In his usual practical, pragmatic way, President Brigham Young gave sound counsel on this matter:

> Some of the brethren come to me and say, "Brother Brigham, is it my duty to pray when I have not one particle of the spirit of prayer in me?" True, at times, men are perplexed and full of care and trouble, . . . [and] a thousand things perplex them; yet our judgment teaches us that it is our duty to pray, whether we are particularly in the spirit of praying or not. My doctrine is, it is your duty to pray; and when the time for prayer comes, John should say, "This is the place and this is the time to pray; knees bend down upon the floor, and do so at once." But John said, "I do not want to pray; I do not feel like it." Knees get down, I say; and down bend the knees, and he begins to think and reflect. Can you say anything? Can you not say, God have mercy on me a sinner? Yes, he can do this, if he can rise up and curse his neighbor for some ill deeds. Now, John, open your mouth and say, Lord, have mercy upon me. "But I do not feel the spirit of prayer." That does not excuse you, for you know what your duty is. You have a passion, a will, a temper to

overcome. You are subject to temptation as other men; and when you are tempted, let the judgment which God has placed within you and the intelligence he has given you by the light of the Spirit be the master in this case.

If I could not master my mouth, I would my knees, and make them bend until my mouth would speak. . . . Let the will of man be brought into subjection to the law of Christ—to all the ordinances of the house of God. What, in his darkness and depression? Yes; for that is the time to prove whether one is a friend of God, that the confidence of the Almighty may increase in his Son. We should so live that our confidence and faith may increase in him. We must even go further than that. Let us so live that the faith and confidence of our Heavenly Father may increase towards us, until he shall know that we will be true to him under any and all circumstances and at all times. When in our darkness and temptation we are found faithful to our duty, that increases the confidence of our God in us. He sees that we will be his servants.

(*Discourses of Brigham Young,* 45).

As President Young said, "You will find that those who wait till the Spirit bids them pray, will never pray much on this earth" (ibid., 44). Prayer helps us to submit our will to that of God, while at the same time acknowledging Him as the fount of every blessing in our lives.

Submission to God's will—"Not my will, but thine" (Luke 22:42)—that is the key, not just to surviving mental illness, but to finding that peace and acceptance that will lead each of us back to our Father's house. Learning that lesson—and it can be a hard one to learn, and is at best a stern struggle—enabled the Prophet Joseph Smith to rise to a higher purpose and privilege: "My son, peace be unto thy soul; thine adversity and thine afflictions shall be but a small moment; And then, if thou endure it well, God shall exalt thee on high" (D&C 121:7–8).

Why is it so hard to bow our knees and our wills to God? King Benjamin explained: "For the natural man is an enemy to God, and has been from the fall of Adam, and will be, forever and ever, unless he yields to the enticings of the Holy Spirit, and putteth off the natural man and becometh a saint through the atonement of Christ the Lord, and becometh as a child, submissive, meek, humble, patient, full of love, willing to submit to all things which the Lord seeth fit to inflict upon him, even as a child doth submit to his father" (Mosiah 3:19).

It is, then, the natural man, with his sensuality and selfishness, who gets in the way of our submission to God. The natural man resists taking the way to the disciple's path. We must not just get around him, but actually banish him from our lives. After all, there is no way to get *around* life; we must get *through* it, and that requires defeating the natural man and becoming submissive, meek, humble, patient, and full of love.

Such submission does not in any way imply witless, blind, ignorant obedience. Yielding our will to God, consecrating our lives to Him and to His service, represents the very antithesis of compulsion or brutish resignation to fate. Our obedience must be freely given, not out of any sense of quid pro quo, not because we expect to gain from what must become a progressive partnership with Deity, but solely because we love God and wish to do His will and to have His purposes paramount in our lives. We could not submit to God, give our whole heart to Him, if we could not trust Him. But we *can* trust Him, not just because He is our Father, but because He possesses all truth, love, knowledge, power, and justice. He is unchanging from everlasting to everlasting. All of His children have equal privileges before Him, for "all are alike unto God" (2 Nephi 26:33). Such knowledge, the Prophet Joseph Smith explained, "does away doubt, and makes faith exceedingly strong" (*Lectures on Faith*, 42).

As we walk hand in hand with the Almighty along the disciple's path through life, ever seeking to become more like Him, our understanding of His purpose for us continually increases: "For he will give unto the faithful line upon line, precept upon precept" (D&C 98:12). That understanding increases as we read and ponder the sacred scriptures and the words of the living prophets. It increases as we partake of saving and exalting ordinances and covenants. And it increases perhaps most of all as we contemplate the infinite atonement of Him who is our Advocate with the Father. God did not spare His Only Begotten Son from suffering and anguish so stark and severe as to cause Jesus to "tremble because of pain, and to bleed at every pore, and to suffer both body and spirit" (D&C 19:18). Why then should *we* despair or rail against the unfairness of life? Jesus, our Advocate, knows perfectly our suffering and helps us through whatever ordeals face us. The prophet Alma spoke adoringly of Christ's compassion for us in our infirmities:

"And he shall go forth, suffering pains and afflictions and temptations of every kind; and this that the word might be fulfilled which saith he will take upon him the pains and the sicknesses of his people. And he will take upon him death, that he may loose the bands of death which bind his people; and he will take upon him their infirmities, that his bowels may be filled with mercy, according to the flesh, that he may know according to the flesh how to succor his people according to their infirmities" (Alma 7:11, 12).

The faith in Christ and the Father that is necessary for us to gain spiritual submissiveness helps us to understand that we cannot expect immunity from the vicissitudes of mortality, the afflictions which are "common to man" (1 Corinthians 10:13). We come to recognize that as Jesus "learned . . . obedience by the things which he suffered" (Hebrews 5:8), so too must we. The trials of mental illness, for example—trials which "trieth [our] patience and [our] faith" (Mosiah 23:21)—will in the long run be understood as having been for our good. They represent the "customized challenges and tutoring that require an added and special submissiveness," in Elder Neal A. Maxwell's felicitous phrase (*One More Strain of Praise,* 13).

As we struggle to become more submissive to God—to freely cede to Him a portion of our moral agency—we must recognize that the enemy of truth—Satan, the great deceiver—will do all in his diabolic power to turn us away from God, convince us to abandon our belief that God loves us, persuade us to "curse God, and die" (Job 2:9), tempt us to lose faith in His power and deny His very existence. He will tempt us to turn on ourselves in the storm of our mental and physical ailments, inviting us to denigrate, demean, and debase our character; to personalize his cankering, malignant misinformation until our souls are filled with his darkness and all hope has been erased. The devil and his works are abroad in the world, perhaps as never before. These wise words of President Brigham Young remind us of that:

"It was revealed to me in the commencement of this Church, that the Church would spread, prosper, grow and extend, and that in proportion to the spread of the Gospel among the nations of the earth, so would the power of Satan rise" (*Journal of Discourses* 13:280).

President Ezra Taft Benson emphasized Satan's role in a darkening world: "As the showdown between good and evil approaches with its accompanying trials and tribulations, Satan is increasingly striving to overcome the Saints with despair, discouragement, despondency, and depression" ("Do Not Despair," 2).

Those who suffer from mental illness, who are burdened with pain, depression, and confusion, must, I believe, be especially on their guard against the wiles of the adversary and his legions of dupes and devils. So too must the circle of loving caregivers around those who are so afflicted.

Our love of God and our spiritual submissiveness to Him increases and our own suffering subsides as we serve others. In a way, service is an antidote for suffering. President Gordon B. Hinckley has commented on this matter: "The best antidote I know for worry is work. The best medicine for despair is service. The best cure for weariness is the challenge of helping someone who is even more tired" (*Stand a Little Taller*, 96). President Hinckley has also pointed out the relationship between service and happiness: "Generally speaking, the most miserable people I know are those who are obsessed with themselves; the happiest people I know are those who lose themselves in the service of others. By and large, I have come to see that if we complain about life, it is because we are thinking only of ourselves" (ibid., 90).

Service to others is the highest expression of Christian stewardship, the hallmark of the lives of the disciples of Christ.

It drives out selfishness, the enemy of spirituality. By subduing the ego, service permits our souls to grow and signifies the extent of our devotion to Christ and His cause. It is the mark of true greatness of character. Jesus knew that: "Whosoever will be great among you, let him be your minister; and whosoever will be chief among you, . . . let him be your servant" (Matthew 20:26–27).

The time spent in service to others leaves less time for the trap of morbid introspection and the snares of the obsessive preoccupation with self that can intensify the suffering inherent in mental illness (and many of its associated maladies). Our own pain and suffering, grievous though they are, somehow become lessened as we reach out to bind up the wounds and dry the tears of those who also are in sorrow and despair. And in the process, our own wounds heal, even if just a little.

But perhaps most importantly, service to others signifies our willingness to submit our will to that of God and binds us closer to Him. King Benjamin knew that when he proclaimed, "When ye are in the service of your fellow beings ye are only in the service of your God" (Mosiah 2:17).

President Marion G. Romney understood well the importance of service and its associated sacrifice in obtaining the peace of heart and soul we all long for:

"When earth life is over and things appear in their true perspective, we shall more clearly see and realize what the Lord and his prophets have repeatedly told us, that the fruits of the gospel are the only objectives worthy of life's full efforts. Their possessor obtains true wealth—wealth in the Lord's view of values. . . . I conceive the blessings of the gospel to be of such inestimable worth that the price for them must be very exacting, and if I correctly understand what the Lord has said on the subject, it is. The price, however, is within the reach of us all, because it is not to be paid in money nor in any of this world's goods but in righteous living. What is required is wholehearted devotion to the gospel and unreserved allegiance to the Church of Jesus Christ of Latter-day Saints. . . . There can be no . . . reservation. We must be willing to sacrifice everything. Through self-discipline and devotion we must demonstrate to the Lord that we are willing to serve him under all circumstances. When we have done this, we shall receive an assurance that we shall have eternal life in the world to come. Then we shall have peace in this world" (in Conference Report, October 1949, 39, 43–44).

As we submit our will to that of God, we find that we are never alone. We can turn to Jesus, our "guardian, guide, and stay," our ever-present friend. We can talk to Him, and He will understand, for He has felt the same pain, the same sorrow we feel. "With His stripes we are healed" (Isaiah 53:5). Through His atonement, He has paid the price to personally know the depths to which our souls may plunge at times. He has searched out these depths that He may know more perfectly how to personally succor us through the seasons of our trials. He knows all there is to know about loneliness; we cannot teach *Him* anything about that, whatever our own condition may be. Yet in our loneliness we are not alone. He will bear us up, perhaps in ways that we cannot at this time realize, gently tending to our souls.

Daniel Defoe's *Robinson Crusoe,* although first published more than two-and-a-half centuries ago, remains a great tribute to the power of the human spirit to overcome adversity. As the sole survivor of a ship caught in a storm and broken apart on a reef near an uninhabited island somewhere off the South

American coast, Crusoe had every reason to believe he had been abandoned by God. Washed ashore by the ocean currents, he managed not only to survive but to build a life for himself, using a mixture of materials found on the island and those he could salvage from the wreck.

At first, Crusoe, alone on his island, bereft of all human companionship, was overcome by loneliness, self-pity, and deep depression. Then he underwent a kind of metamorphosis:

"I had a dismal prospect of my condition, for as I was not cast away upon that island without being driven, as is said, by a violent storm quite out of the course of our intended voyage, and a great way, viz., some hundreds of leagues, out of the ordinary course of the trade of mankind, I had great reason to consider it as a determination of Heaven, that in this desolate place, and in this desolate manner, I should end my life; the tears would run plentifully down my face when I made these reflections; and sometimes I would expostulate with myself why Providence should thus completely ruin its creatures and render them so absolutely miserable; so abandoned without help, so entirely depressed, that it could hardly be rational to be thankful for such a life" (*Robinson Crusoe*, 44–45).

Later, however, Crusoe found first solace and then deep faith in his study of the Bible, copies of which he located in a seaman's chest salvaged from the wreck. He began to pray, for the first time in his life, and to reflect upon the "many wonderful mercies which [his] solitary condition was attended with" (78). He began to give thanks to God, "who had thus spread [his, Crusoe's] table in the wilderness" (90). Wrote he, "I learned here again to observe, that it is very rare that the providence of God casts us into any condition of life so low, or any misery so great, but we may see something or other to be thankful for, and may see others in worse circumstances than our own" (ibid., 130). Challenges became tests of worthiness for the castaway.

Crusoe found peace when he put his hand in the hand of God and walked with Him.

That, then, is my message: Where can we turn for peace, amidst the pain and suffering, the loneliness, depression, and despair of mental illness? It matters not whether we are the primary sufferer or those secondary sufferers who share the burden of sorrow. The answer is the same: Reach out to God. Give your life to Him. Thank Him daily that He loves you enough to permit you to undergo tutorial suffering. Submit your will to His. Be obedient. Keep the commandments. Recognize that the fire of affliction, which scars and diminishes some souls, purifies and ennobles others, transforming them into celestial creatures filled with supernal joy.

Never forget: "All your losses will be made up to you in the resurrection, provided you continue faithful. By the vision of the Almighty I have seen it," said the Prophet Joseph Smith, who knew more about anguish, disappointment, and spiritual affliction than most (*History of the Church*, 5:362).

The renowned poet Emma Lou Thayne has written about the only sure foundation upon which peace can be built in the face of the tears and turmoil of mental illness. Sister Thayne knows from firsthand experience whereof she speaks. She poured out the anguish of her soul as she struggled to assist a beloved daughter, Becky, suffering from bipolar disorder, bulimia, and anorexia (see Thayne, "Search for Inner Peace is Universal," 5). Thankfully, Becky has recovered, after years of desperate struggle, though she still must take medication daily.

Mother and daughter have chronicled that struggle in an inspiring book, fittingly titled *Hope and Recovery*. Oh, how I long for the day when all who have such stories to tell can record similar victories! Sister Thayne's words of hope and peace provide a fitting capstone on this book. They are as follows:

> Where can I turn for peace? Where is my solace
> When other sources cease to make me whole?
> When with a wounded heart, anger, or malice,
> I draw myself apart, Searching my soul?
>
> Where, when my aching grows,
> Where, when I languish,
> Where, in my need to know, where can I run?
> Where is the quiet hand to calm my anguish?
> Who, who can understand? He, only One.
>
> He answers privately, Reaches my reaching
> In my Gethsemane, Savior and Friend.
> Gentle the peace he finds for my beseeching.
> Constant he is and kind, Love without end.
> (*Hymns,* no. 129)

FOR ADDITIONAL
INFORMATION

- *The Diagnostic and Statistical Manual of Mental Disorders, Fourth Edition* (Washington, DC: American Psychiatric Association, 1994) is the standard guide to clinical practice in mental illness. It is widely used by physicians, psychologists, social workers, and many other mental health professionals. I have referred to it often in preparing this book.
- *The National Institute of Mental Health* (NIMH) produces many free publications of value to the general public on the topic of mental illnesses. They include the following, not in any particular order:
  "Anxiety Disorders"
  "Depression"
  "Depression: What Every Woman Should Know"
  "Eating Disorders"
  "Bipolar Disorder"
  "A Story of Bipolar Disorder" (manic-depression illness)
  "Schizophrenia"
  "Medications"

These publications may be ordered from the National Institute of Mental Health, Information & Inquiries Branch, 6001 Executive Boulevard, Room 8184, MSC 9663, Bethesda, MD 20892-9663.

- LDS Family Services is a corporation that exists to serve Church members and others. It provides advice and service on mental health concerns consistent with gospel principles. Persons usually are referred to Family Services by their bishop.
- www.ldsmentalhealth.org is a non-profit, volunteer corporation providing free resources to LDS ecclesiastical leaders, Church members, and the general public concerning mental illness and other social/emotional concerns. It is not sponsored by The Church of Jesus Christ of Latter-day Saints, nor is it an organization of the Church. However, the website provides a great wealth of reliable, gospel-compatible information on a broad variety of mental illnesses. Much of the information is taken from talks by General Authorities and faithful LDS professionals in the mental health field. The information is not intended to replace the spiritual direction of ecclesiastical leaders and does not provide directions on medication or counseling of mentally ill persons.
- Survivors of suicide will get much information, inspiration, and understanding from the book by Jaynann M. Payne and Dr. Rick Hawkes, titled *Where Is Our Hope for Peace? A Resource for LDS Families Coping with Suicide,* (Ogden, Utah: Hidden Treasures Institute, 2001).
- Elder M. Russell Ballard's book *Suicide: Some Things We Know, and Some We Do Not* (Salt Lake City: Deseret Book Company, 1993) will provide comfort to Latter-day Saints who are struggling in the aftermath of suicide.

BIBLIOGRAPHY

Ballard, M. Russell. "Suicide: Some Things We Know, and Some We Do Not." *Ensign,* October 1987.

Benson, Ezra Taft. "Do Not Despair." *Ensign,* October 1986.

Bryson, Amy Joi. "Mental Illness Hijacks Families." *Deseret News,* 19 May 2002.

Cannon, George Q. *Gospel Truth.* Salt Lake City: Deseret Book, 1987.

Defoe, Daniel. *Robinson Crusoe.* New York: Barnes and Noble, 1996.

"Depression in Children—Part I." *The Harvard Mental Health Letter,* February 2002.

Durant, Will. *The Story of Philosophy.* New York: Simon & Schuster, 1927.

Gorman, Jack M., M. D. *The Essential Guide to Mental Health.* New York: St. Martin Press, 1998.

Hales, Dianne, and Dr. Robert E. Hales. "When a Teenager Is Sad . . . Pay Attention!" *Parade Magazine,* 5 May 2002.

Hanks, Marion D. *Bread upon the Waters.* Salt Lake City: Bookcraft, 1991.

Hilton, Sterling C., Gilbert W. Fellingham, and Joseph L. Lyon. "Suicide Rates and Religious Commitment in Young Adult Males in Utah." *American Journal of Epidemiology* 155, no. 5.

Hinckley, Gordon B. "Personal Worthiness to Exercise the Priesthood." *Ensign,* May 2002.

―――. *Stand a Little Taller.* Salt Lake City: Deseret Book, 2001.

Hymns of The Church of Jesus Christ of Latter-day Saints. Salt Lake City: The Church of Jesus Christ of Latter-day Saints, 1985.

Journal of Discourses. 26 vols. London: Latter-day Saints' Book Depot, 1854–86.

Kimball, Spencer W. *Teachings of Spencer W. Kimball.* Edited by Edward Kimball. Salt Lake City: Bookcraft, 1982.

―――. *Tragedy or Destiny?* Salt Lake City: Deseret Book, 1977.

Kübler-Ross, Elisabeth. *On Death and Dying.* New York: Simon & Schuster, 1997.

Kushner, Harold. *When Bad Things Happen to Good People.* New York: Avon Books, 1981.

―――. "You Don't Have to Be Perfect to Be Loved." *Parade Magazine,* 8 September 1996.

Lewis, C. S. *Mere Christianity.* New York: Macmillan, 1960.

Lindbergh, Anne Morrow. *Time,* 5 February 1973.

Manchester, William. *The Last Lion.* London: Sphere Books Ltd., 1984.

Maxwell, Neal A. *All These Things Shall Give Thee Experience.* Salt Lake City: Deseret Book, 1980.

―――. "Content with the Things Allotted unto Us." *Ensign,* May 2000.

———. "Notwithstanding My Weakness." *Ensign,* November 1976.

———. *One More Strain of Praise.* Salt Lake City: Bookcraft, 1999.

McConkie, Bruce R. *Mormon Doctrine.* Salt Lake City: Bookcraft, 1966.

Montgomery, Lucy Maud. *Anne of Green Gables.* New York: Avenel Books, 1985.

Morrison, Mary. "Light in Darkness." *Ensign,* June 1998.

Oxford Dictionary of Quotations, The. 3d ed. Oxford: Oxford University Press, 1987.

Packer, Boyd K. "Children." *Ensign,* May 2002.

———. "Little Children." *Ensign,* November 1986.

———. "Solving Emotional Problems in the Lord's Own Way." *Ensign,* May 1978.

———. "The Edge of the Light." *BYU Today,* March 1991.

Pinborough, Jan Underwood. "Mental Illness: In Search of Understanding and Hope." *Ensign,* February 1989.

Romney, Marion G. Conference Report, October 1949.

Schwartz, Jeffrey M., M. D. *Brain Lock.* New York: Harper Collins Publishers, 1996.

Schwartz, Jeffrey M., and Sharon Begley. *The Mind and the Brain: Neuroplasticity and the Power of Mental Force.* New York: Regan Books, 2002.

Smith, Joseph. *History of The Church of Jesus Christ of Latter-day Saints.* Edited by B. H. Roberts. 7 vols. 2d ed. rev. Salt Lake City: The Church of Jesus Christ of Latter-day Saints, 1932–51.

———. *Lectures on Faith.* Salt Lake City: Deseret Book, 1985.

Smith, Joseph F. *Gospel Doctrine.* Salt Lake City: Deseret Book, 1986.

Smith, Joseph Fielding. *Doctrines of Salvation.* 3 vols. Compiled by Bruce R. McConkie. Salt Lake City: Deseret Book, 1954–56.

———. *Selections from Doctrines of Salvation.* Salt Lake City: The Church of Jesus Christ of Latter-day Saints, 2001.

"Stigma: Building Awareness and Understanding about Mental Illness." National Mental Health Association, March 2001.

Styron, William. *Darkness Visible.* London: Picador, 1991.

Sullivan, Clyde E. "Suicide." In *Encyclopedia of Mormonism.* 4 vols. Edited by Daniel H. Ludlow. New York: Macmillan, 1992.

Thayne, Emma Lou. "Search for Inner Peace Is Universal." *Church News,* 29 December 2001.

Thayne, Emma Lou, and Becky Thayne Markosian. *Hope and Recovery.* Haverford, Pa.: InfinityPublishing.com, 2001.

Weaver, Sarah Jane. "Mackenzie's Dance." *Church News,* 27 April 2002.

Winthrop, Robert C. *The Life and Letters of John Winthrop: Governor of the Massachussetts-Bay Company at Their Immigration to New England, 1630.* 3d ed. Boston: Little, Brown & Company, 1869.

Wolpert, Lewis. *Malignant Sadness: The Anatomy of Depression.* London: The Free Press, 1999.

Young, Brigham. *Discourses of Brigham Young.* Salt Lake City: Deseret Book, 1978.

INDEX

Abuse, child, 57–59

Acceptance, nonjudgmental, 21, 23, 26–27

Accountability, 102–3

Agency, 12

Aging, 112

Agoraphobia, 37, 40–41

Alma the Younger, 19–20, 111

Anorexia nervosa: examples of, 83–88; symptoms of, 86–88; causes of, 88; treatment for, 89–90

Anti-depressants: effectiveness of, 36, 56–57, 63; for postpartum depression, 65; for bulimia, 97

Anxiety, beneficial, 31–32

Anxiety disorder, generalized, 35–36

Anxiety disorders: as category, xii; pain of, 2; statistics on, 32–33; types of, 33–35

Atonement, 13–14, 120–21, 127

Atypical depression, 55

Ballard, M. Russell, 114

Benson, Ezra Taft, 129

Binge eating, 95–97

Biological causes: of panic attacks, 38; of obsessive-compulsive behavior, 46; of bipolar disorder, 52; of depression, 56; of schizophrenia, 77

Bipolar disorder, 21, 52

Bishops: discern sin from mental illness, 20, 24; do not assume roles of mental health professionals, 25, 111–12

Blame: of patients for their mental illness, 4–5; for suffering, 14; causes unnecessary suffering, 24–25; as warning sign of depression, 61; for suicides, 100–101, 114

Blood phobia, 34

Body image, 86–87, 90–91, 96

Brain abnormalities, 77–78

Brain function, 88

Brain Lock, 44–45
Breastfeeding, 65
Bulimia, 95–97
Burns, Robert, 14

Cannon, George Q., 101
Chemical imbalances, xiii–xiv. *See also* Biological causes, Genetic influences
Children: mental illness in, 28; depression in, 57–63; take blame for parent's suicide, 114
Christianity, 14–15
Church leaders, 21
Church of Jesus Christ of Latter-day Saints, The, members of: blame victim, 4; mental health issues of, 66–69, 91–94, 106; suicide funerals of, 113
Churchill, Winston, 49
Cognitive behavioral therapy: for obsessive-compulsive disorders, xv, xvi, 46; effectiveness of, 29; for depression in youth, 63, 73; with bulimics, 97
Comparisons, 67
Compassion, 21, 23, 26–27, 117
Compulsions, 43–45
Consequences, 19–20
Control, 88, 96
Creation, 11
Cromwell, Oliver, 50

Death: of parent, 57–58; from starvation, 88; preparations for, 108–9; dealing with suicide, 112–14
Deceit, 87–88
Defoe, Daniel, 131–33
Delusions, 54–55, 76

Dementias, xii–xiii
Demonic possession, 23
Dependency, drug, 36

Depression: suicide rate from, xiii, 2, 51, 99, 107; world statistics on, 1, 50; pain of, 2; sufferers of, 4, 28, 49–50; during repentance process, 20; treatment for, 27–28; in children and youth, 28, 57–63; with generalized anxiety disorder, 36; with panic disorders, 38, 41–42; symptoms of, 50–51; types of, 51–52, 54–55; examples of, 52–54; origins of, 55–57; warning signs of, in children, 61; in women, 63–64; postpartum type of, 64–65; in LDS women, 65–69; in Mary Morrison, 69–74; in bulimics, 96–97
Diana, Princess of Wales, 95
Discernment, 20–21
Disinterest, 61
Divorce, 57–58
Dopamine, 77
Durrant, Will, 122
Dysthymia, 55

Eagleton, Thomas, 4
Eating disorders: category of, xiii; examples of, 83–86; anorexia nervosa as, 86–95; bulimia as, 95–97
Electro-convulsive therapy (ECT), 70–71, 74
Emotional numbing, 46–47
Endurance, 118–20

Eternal life, 121, 130–31
Eternity, 123
Exercise, fanatical, 87, 96
Exorcism, 23

Faith: crises of, 17–18; complete
    healing through, 25; to
    overcome depression, 68; to be
    submissive to life's trials, 118,
    128
Family: help from, xix–xx;
    blaming of, 5; can help
    anorectics, 89, 91, 94–95
Fear: beneficial type of, 31–32; in
    panic attack, 37, 72; in
    anorectics, 88
Firearms, 109
First Presidency (1834), 8
Flashbacks, 34–35, 46–47
Foolishness, 14
Foreknowledge, 8–9, 12
Fuller, Adrie, 95
Fuller, Mackenzie, 90, 95
Funerals, 113

Genetic influences: of mental
    illness, xiv; on depression, 50,
    56; on schizophrenia, 77
God: love of, xviii–xix; perspective
    of, 7; omniscience of, 7–9, 12,
    16; permits trials and
    tribulations, 15–16; is sole
    judge of mentally ill, 103–5;
    putting trust in, 118–19,
    125–26, 131; trusts us, 125
Gore, Tipper, 28
Gorman, Jack M., 51, 77–78
Grief, 113

Hales, Diana, 59–61

Hales, Robert E., 59–61
Hallucinations, 3, 75–76
Hanks, Marion D., 104
Happiness, 129
Harvest, law of, 14, 19
Heart problems, 84, 88, 96
Hilton, Sterling C., 106
Hinckley, Gordon B.: on child
    abuse, 58–59; on wife abuse,
    63–64; on service, 129
Holy Ghost, 20–21
Hospitalization, 78, 84–85,
    88–89
Hostility, 108
House, analogy of, 11–12
Hughes, Howard, 45

Illness, severe, 108
Inadequacy, 93
Intellectual function, 77, 88
Interpersonal rejection sensitivity,
    55

Jesus Christ: knew of plan of
    salvation, 9–10; has power to
    heal, 25; turning to, in times of
    suffering, 66, 69, 73, 122,
    125–27, 134; suffering of, 120,
    127, 131
Job, 5–6
Judgment, 4–5, 102–5

Kimball, Spencer W.: on accepting
    mortality, 13; on suicide, 101,
    105
Kubler-Ross, Elisabeth, 113
Kuehnl, Sharlene, 53–54
Kushner, Harold S., 8–9, 94

Lectures on Faith, 7–8

Lee, Robert E., 50
Lee, Harold B., 12–13
Lewis, C. S., 11–12
Lewis, Meriwether, 50
Librium, 36
Lincoln, Abraham, 50
Lindburgh, Anne Morrow, 16
Loneliness, 108
Luther, Martin, 50

MacKay, David O., 12–13
Major depression, 51–52
Manchester, William, 49
Marriage, 68
Maxwell, Neal A.: on God's perspective, 7; on trials in mortality, 68, 121; on feelings of inadequacy, 93; on customized challenges, 128
McConkie, Bruce R., 101–2
Medication: effectiveness of, xv, 28–29, 115–16; faith does not negate need for, 18; anti-depressant types of, 36, 56–57, 73; side effects of, 71; for schizophrenia, 78; for bulimia, 97
Memory, repressed, 47
Memory loss, 71, 88
Menstruation, 84, 87
Mental health, 116
Mental illness: definition of, xii; is not a punishment, 16–17, 20; no shame or guilt for having, 23–24; is not caused by lack of willpower, 26; as not dangerous to others, 27; is treatable, 28–29; as customized challenge, 128
Montgomery, Lucy Maud, 123

Mood changes, 61
Mood congruent, 54–55
Mood disorders, xii
Morrison, Mary, 38–42, 69–74
Mortality: as time of learning, 11; suffering as part of, 13–14; lacking perspective on, 122
Moses, xix

Nash, John, 75, 77
Natural laws, 15
Natural man, 126
Neglect, child, 57–59
Neurotransmitters, xiv, 56, 77–78
Norepinephrine, 56

Obedience, 126
Obsessions, 42–44
Obsessive-compulsive disorder (OCD): cognitive-behavioral therapy helps, xv–xvi; symptoms of, 2, 34, 42–46; as common to bulimia patients, 96–97
Omniscience, of God, 7–9, 12, 16
Opposition, 22

Packer, Boyd K.: on walking into darkness, 12–13; on responsibility for children, 59; on accepting struggles in life, 67–68; on changing behavior, 101, 110–11
Pain, 115
Panic disorders: description of, 36–38; example of, 38–42
Paranoid delusions, 76
Patience, 119
Patriarchal blessing, 40
Peace, 133

Perfection, 92–94

Perfectionism, 66, 85, 91

Persecution, 14–15

Perspective, of God, 7, 122

Pharmacogenetics, xiv

Phobias, social, 33

Phobias, specific, 33

Phobic avoidance, 37–38, 72

Pinborough, Jan Underwood, 57, 80–81

Plan of salvation, 13

Positron emission tomography (PET), xv–xvi

Postpartum depression, 64–65

Post-traumatic stress disorder, 34–35, 46–47

Prayer: seeking answers to, 18, 40, 117; to overcome depression, 62, 68; while in despair, 124–26

Predispositions, 38, 46. *See also* Biological causes

Priesthood blessings, 25, 62

Professional help, 18, 20, 62

Psychiatrists, xvi–xvii

Psychopharmacology, 115

Psychosis, 3, 54–55, 65, 75

Psychotherapists, xvi–xvii

Psychotherapy: effectiveness of, xv, 29; for postpartum depression, 65; for schizophrenia, 78

Punishment, 16–17, 20

Relationships, dysfunctional, 108

Relief Society, 67

Religious commitment, 106

Remorse, 20

Repentance, 20

Repetitive behaviors, 43

Restoration, doctrine of, 111

Revelation, personal, 68

Righteousness, 21–22

Rituals, 43

Robinson Crusoe, 131–33

Romney, Marion G., 130–31

Rumination, 54

Sadness, 50

Satan, 23, 128

Scharman, Brent, 66

Schizophrenia: category of, xii; psychotic symptoms of, 3, 75–76; negative symptoms of, 76–78; examples of, 78–81

School problems, 61

Schwartz, Jeffrey M., xv–xvi, 44–45

Self-acceptance, 67–68, 89

Self-confidence, 72–73

Self-criticism, 61

Self-worth, 90–91, 93–95

Serotonin, 56, 77

Service, 129–30

Shadrach, Meshach, and Abed–nego, 118

Sherman, William T., 50

Sin: causes suffering, 14, 19–20; may cause mental illness, 16–17

Sleep problems, 61, 71

Smith, Joseph: on suffering and sin, 4–5; feels forsaken, 6; on Christ's knowledge, 9–10; on torment of man, 16–17; on progression beyond the grave, 92, 133; on adversity, 125–26; on man's trust in God, 127

Smith, Joseph F., 14–15

Smith, Joseph Fielding, 9, 92–93

Sock School of Psychiatry, 26

Sorensen, Terrell, 78–80

Starvation, 88
Stigmas, social, 3–4, 29, 117
Stock, Rob, 52–53
Stress, extreme, 107–8
Styron, William, 1–2
Submissiveness, to God: to survive trials, 118, 125–28; service signifies, 129–31
Substance abuse: makes depression worse, 63; in bulimics, 96–97; as warning sign for suicide, 107
Suffering: understanding God's will in, 6–7; time perspective of, 10; as part of mortality, 13, 121; causes of, 14–16, 20; of all associated with mental illness, 115; of Christ, 120
Suicide: of depression patients, xiii, 51, 99–100; of teenagers, 59; of schizophrenics, 78; Church teachings on, 100–5, 113; statistics on, 106–7; warning signs of, 107–9; talking about, 109–12; aftermath of, 112–14
Supportive therapy, 29

Talk therapy, xv, 116. *See also* Psychotherapy
Tardive dyskinesia, 71
Thayne, Becky, 133
Thayne, Emma Lou, 133–34
Thought disorders, 20, 76
Time, perspectives on, 10
Tolstoy, Leo, 50
Trust, in God, 12, 118–19, 126–27

Understanding, 21, 23, 26–27
Unhappiness, 4–5

Vagus nerve, 34
Valium, 36
Verbal warnings, 108
Violence, 27, 81–82
Von Bismarck, Otto, 50
Von Goethe, Johann, 50

Wallace, Mike, 28
Washing of hands, 43
Weaknesses, 122
Weaver, Sarah Jane, 90
Weight problems, 61, 71. *See also* Eating Disorders
"Where Can I Turn for Peace?," 134
Wicked, 14
Wife abuse, 63–64
Willpower, 26–27
Winthrop, Robert C., xx
Wolpert, Lewis, 2
Women, 63–64, 66–69, 106
Wordsworth, William, 123
World Health Organization (WHO), 1

Young, Brigham: on endurance, 119–20; on prayer, 124–25; on rise of Satan, 128–29
Youth: mental illness of, 28; depression in, 57–63; suicides of, 59, 106, 110–11; eating disorders in, 86, 91

ABOUT THE AUTHOR

Alexander B. Morrison was sustained to the First Quorum of the Seventy of The Church of Jesus Christ of Latter-day Saints in April 1987 and was named emeritus General Authority in October 2000. With master's degrees from the University of Alberta and the University of Michigan and a doctorate from Cornell University, he is an internationally respected scientist who has directed several committees in the World Health Organization. In 1984 he became the first recipient of the David M. Kennedy Service Award from the Kennedy International Center at Brigham Young University, and in 2001 he was named administrator of the year by the George W. Romney Institute of Public Management at BYU. He and his wife, Shirley Brooks Morrison, are the parents of eight children.